BRUTAL
KINDNESS

BRUTAL KINDNESS

A Guide to using the Power of **Purposeful Positivity** and the **5 HABITS FOR HAPPINESS** to become CLEAR2LEARN and Create a Life that You Love!

By Steven Carvajal

Dedication Page:

To my beautiful wife, Lisa, I love you! Thank you for going on this journey with me!

Contents

"Human greatness does not lie in wealth or power, but in character and goodness. People are just people, and all people have faults and shortcomings, but all of us are born with a basic goodness."

-Anne Frank

Foreword — YOU'RE A GOOD PERSON!

Oh, I know, you're not perfect, but who is?

And, you're right; I don't know you, but so what? I'd rather see the good in you than expect to find something bad. In my experience, people usually rise... or fall to the expectations of those around them.

It seems like these days we're all too ready to hear the worst about people and find out the REAL TRUTH, because we see bad behavior as commonplace and normal. Of course politicians and lawyers are crooked creeps! Of course kids are lazy and selfish! But just because we see that on the news doesn't mean it's true about the majority of us!

In our quest for free will and happiness, we have actually become more and more cynical. Yes, I know some people really do bad things, but does that mean we, as human beings, are bad? Evil? Doomed?

Sadly, what we believe often becomes true. It is becoming common knowledge that we all need to be watched, policed, and monitored because, instead of happiness, too much freedom quickly brings out the worst in us. **Because of our human nature; freedom, not just power, corrupts!**

BUT IT DOESN'T HAVE TO BE THAT WAY!

Here's something better to believe: We are GOOD PEOPLE!

We care, we help, we forgive, and we learn. By learning to think, and more importantly, act that way, we can turn away from our current common knowledge, and create a better way of life!

It's time to examine our own hearts and minds and start to ACT, LIVE, and LOVE like the good, blessed, and fortunate people we really are! It's time to start creating the life and relationships we really want instead of being unhappy and disgruntled with the cards life has dealt us. It's time to learn to be POSITIVE ON PURPOSE!

Over the course of many years and many, many failures, I've been led to and learned the concepts I'll teach in this book. Through reflection, study, and what I can only believe to be divine inspiration, my mind and my heart have changed in such a way that it has allowed me to renew my thinking and transform my life.

I'm not talking about just reading a bunch of books or taking college courses and suddenly I'm perfectly happy! I had to learn the concepts I teach in this book on a spiritual level; learn them to the depths of my soul because knowing how one should live and actually living that way are two very different things!

I wish I could go back and talk to me at the age of 15 when I was a freshman in high school so I could have made A's and B's instead of C's and D's! I wish I had this book to read before I spent ten years procrastinating my way through college, or before my first marriage fell apart, but I can't change the past.

It took me many years to learn how to **FORGIVE** the past and focus on a good and happy present and future. With this book, you can learn to do the same much faster!

While I am a really good teacher, keep in mind, I'm not a genius!

I don't claim to have invented or own the rights to any of the concepts that I've used to turn my life around or that I've written about. I'm sure many of these concepts have long, Latin-based psychological terms or medical names, and were researched and accepted long before I was born. I may well have read or heard about them somewhere, but I only teach from things I've worked out in my mind and have used in my life: I'm only trying to teach these practices and ways of thinking because they've worked for me and they're working for my students!

I'm now a successful and happily married high school teacher, father, speaker, mentor, and a budding writer. I also use what I've learned to teach my students how to be happier and more successful, too!

3

Because of what I teach them and how I treat them, it's not uncommon for me to hear, "Thank you, Mr. Carvajal! You're the only reason I graduated." "Thank you, Mr. Carvajal! You're the only one who believed in me."

I couldn't be that kind of teacher if I was still focused on everything that was wrong with me. I couldn't consistently be doing good in the world if I still let my negative beliefs, emotions, and habits control me. I had to change my thinking and recreate who I am and what my purpose is.

I hope that's why you're here! Happiness, success, and fulfilling relationships are what we all want; and the truths, habits, and ways of thinking and acting that are clearly explained and detailed in this book can really help you do that!

You're already reading this, so you're probably a pretty open-minded person and because of that, this book can and will be very valuable to you. I've put a lot of love and thought into it and I'm glad to offer it to you! I hope you'll accept it and keep learning with me!

Regardless of whether you read on or not, thank you for reading this far! Thank you for taking a risk. I promise that I will do my best to ensure that your faith in me is not in vain.

Sincerely,

Steve Carvajal

"Anyone who stops learning is old, whether at twenty or eighty. Anyone who keeps learning stays young. The greatest thing in life is to keep your mind young."

-Henry Ford

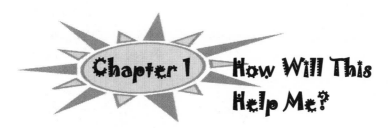

Chapter 1 — How Will This Help Me?

That depends on you!

Too many people will not admit they have an issue they need help with because they're afraid of being judged, but I'm NOT here to do that! I'm here to help you get what you want, not make you feel bad or do anything you don't want to do! For this book to help you, you're going to need to be honest with yourself!

Take a moment and think: Where in your life are you struggling?

What are the issues that trouble you and steal your joy? All I ask is that you be honest with yourself in your heart. If you find these questions upsetting, be kind and **FORGIVE** yourself for past mistakes... and me for asking these questions!

I'm NOT going to ask you to remember your struggles and mistakes so you'll feel bad or guilty, but rather so you can focus on coming to terms with them and moving beyond them.

As far as I'm concerned, you're a GOOD PERSON and reading this book may well be the first step towards putting negative memories and beliefs where they belong: firmly behind you!

Below are some common issues many of us have struggled with:

Do you struggle with work?

Do you have a boss/coworker/teacher who's a "monster," or an "idiot?" Do you have coworkers or classmates that you can't stand? Do you find your work to be mind-numbingly boring or crazily stressful?

Do you struggle with family and relationships?

Do your kids or parents, or your significant other or spouse stress you out and disappoint you? Do you have family or other people in your life you have to steel yourself to be around or you've broken off contact with because they hurt, aggravate, or annoy you on a regular basis?

Do you have plans or goals that you don't know how to make happen, or you've more or less given up on? Maybe you've had them for years, but you're no closer to making them happen now than you were then; or you use to be passionate about something, but you no longer do it even though it brought you great joy.

Are you shy, or do you fear there's something wrong with you?
Other people don't seem to worry about the things you do or get upset as easily as you do. You get nervous around people and it's a struggle to meet new people. You wish you could be as confident or carefree as other people you know.

If you answered yes to any of those questions, this book can help you!

If you answered yes to ALL OF THEM, then you're just like me!

Okay, Thank God that's over! This book is about **PURPOSEFUL POSITIVITY!** This book is about learning to see you, others, and the world as a place full of potential and goodness! Now let's think about what's possible.

Consider the possibilities: Wouldn't it be great…

- ✓ **If that one extremely annoying person you know…maybe even live with…could actually learn to act differently because you started treating him or her differently?**
- ✓ **If you and your family members became much more successful at work or at school?**
- ✓ **If your dull or antagonistic marriage/relationship became happier and more supportive, or interactions with your ex became calmer and more mutually respectful?**

- ✓ If you had a new sense of purpose and enjoyment in relationships at home, as well as with coworkers and friends?
- ✓ If you learned to accept and love yourself just the way you are, and to focus on your strengths instead of your mistakes or weaknesses?

Literally, all of the above happened to me as I learned to be Positive on Purpose. Actually, they didn't just happen. I caused those changes in my life and relationships because I retrained my thinking. With **PURPOSEFUL POSITIVITY**, I changed my beliefs and actions, and so can you!

BRUTAL KINDNESS Q&A:

Q- "This all seems to be too good to be true and too easy! How do I know this will work for me?"

A- Trust me it's not! Just reading this book or ANY book will <u>NOT</u> make all of the above changes happen! Honest work and being coachable will! If you want positive changes to happen in your life, then you want to do the work!

You have to be the one who decides if you will or not. Nobody can do it for you, but **keep in mind that you don't value what you don't work for!** Do what I ask you to do and you'll see the difference it makes in your life! **Trust me, you're worth the trouble!**

"All truth passes through three stages. First, it is ridiculed. Second, it is violently opposed. Third, it is accepted as being self-evident."

-Arthur Schopenhauer

Chapter 2   Facing the Truth

We are pretty good at seeing the truth about others, but not so good at facing the truth about ourselves! Why is that?

We resist it, we argue it, we try to deny it; and the reality is that as long as we can't admit or face our truths, we also can't do anything about them!

In the classroom, I'm known for being **BRUTALLY KIND!** I'm blunt, straight-talking, almost rudely direct and plain spoken, but I'm also very caring and kind. I once had a student tell me, "You're the nicest mean teacher I've ever had!" I still smile when I think about it!

Being **BRUTALLY KIND** means being tough because you care! It's not nice! Nice says, "It's okay! I know you're doing the best you can; that's just the way you are." Instead, if you were my student and not acting right, I'd look at you like I was going to burn a hole through your head with my eyes, and sometimes that's enough all by itself to get kids back on track!

If needed, I'd also speak to you outside in the hallway and tell you to, **"CUT YOUR CRAP OUT! YOU'RE BETTER THAN THAT! YOU'RE A GOOD PERSON SO START ACTING LIKE IT!"**

I know! You are NOT a student in my class and not everybody needs to be "straightened out." You'll be the judge of that; you ARE a GOOD PERSON and you'll decide how closely you need to read those sections entitled **BRUTAL KINDNESS.**

Put another way, **BRUTAL KINDNESS** is a reminder and demand that you refocus and act like your best self!

Are you wondering who or what is "your best self?"

I mean the way you'd act at a job interview. The way you'd act on a first date, or when you're meeting your boyfriend's or girlfriend's parents for the first time.

You see, the problem is many of us see ourselves differently than the way we'd act in those situations. We think that how we are on an average day with the people we usually spend time with as what's real, but being on our "best behavior" is just an act we put on when we really think something or someone is important.

Actually, **THEY'RE BOTH ACTS!** It's just that our normal behavior is so automatic we think it's the truth.

You think you're just being you, but that's a lie you didn't even know you were telling yourself! **If we want long-term happiness, we've got to learn to separate how we act from who we are.**

So, here's the honest truth: Most of us, in my opinion, lie to ourselves and about ourselves on a regular basis! And, yes, that includes me and you! Of course we don't do it on purpose, **but I've found that the majority of us habitually sneak, lie, and cheat because most of the time we are on autopilot!**

Automatic behavior is hard to change because it is so thoughtless and automatic. Kids don't get up in the morning and think, "I'm going to fail a test, get written up, and sent to the office today!" Newlyweds don't think, "I'm going to cheat on my spouse, fight with my in-laws, and be divorced in a year or two." But that's what many of us do without ever realizing we're doing anything at all! We just think we're living our lives, and sometimes things just don't turn out right, but that's **mostly NOT true!**

If we could all learn to WAKE UP, PUT A SMILE ON OUR FACES, AND <u>ACT RIGHT</u> NO MATTER HOW WE FEEL, our lives would dramatically change for the better!

But it's not that easy, is it?

Actually, it's easier than you think! We've just been focusing on the wrong things! We've all accepted lies that keep us out of balance and unhappy; and until we recognize them and create new and better ways of thinking, we will doom ourselves to making the same mistakes over and over again.

Before we delve further into this, let's do some ground work! I'm going to tell you about some things we **ALL** know to be true that are just **WRONG and some REAL truths we've forgotten about!** Then we'll give ourselves good reasons to do this work! You'll have space to get clear about what you have and what you want, and about where you are now and where you're going.

If we give our minds a proper focus and understanding of what's at stake, it's much easier to do the work when you'd rather be playing video games, on social media, or watching TV.

The first Key to Happiness lies in understanding what happiness really is... and is NOT!

Success is not the key to happiness. Happiness is the key to success. If you love what you are doing, you will be successful.

-Albert Schweitzer

Chapter 3 — **Happiness**

Do you want to know the FIRST (and _WORST!_) _BIG LIE_ that many of us have accepted as the truth?

That we should pursue happiness.

"So, what's wrong with pursuing happiness? Why shouldn't I do my best to get what I want?"

I never said you shouldn't do your best to get what you want! You're always better off doing your best, but that's not how happiness works!

If you have to pursue happiness, that means you're **NOT** happy now because some circumstance is missing in your life and all you have to do is go get it!

As long as we believe that happiness is...
>   -skiing down a mountain
>   -lying on a beach
>   -married to that beautiful man or woman of our
> dreams
>   -driving that brand new, shiny sports car
>   -living in that mansion

...we are destined to be unhappy!

Although we all know on some level that money can't buy happiness, most of us still live as if it can!

Even if what we want is not materialistic and shallow, as long as we are putting conditions on our happiness and postponing it, we are setting ourselves up for more unhappiness!

What the Pursuit of Happiness Really Means

The pursuit of happiness, especially here in the United States, really means **the Pursuit of NEW**; and it can easily become an unhealthy obsession! **For many of us, the thrill of getting new stuff becomes a cheap substitute for real happiness.**

If we are focused on pursuing happiness, we will ALWAYS need more new experiences (vacations, meals at fancy restaurants, crushes/love interests, etc...) and toys (cars, boats, gadgets, clothes, handbags, etc...) because "brand new" doesn't stay new for very long!

In just a few days or weeks after getting something new, the shine will dull and the excitement will fade. We'll soon end up feeling just as dissatisfied and unhappy as we were before, and we'll need another "fix" to make us feel good again.

The Pursuit of NEW also means we don't value and take care of what we have!

It means...

- we're wasting our time fantasizing about a new car instead of washing and waxing the car we have and getting the oil changed.

-we're daydreaming about winning the lotto and rolling in money instead of taking care of our current jobs and customers.

-we're gossiping about the coworkers we don't like instead of discussing our concerns with them or HR, or applying for and getting that promotion or better job.

-Even worse, some of us fantasize about and/or flirt with our next "true love" or think about/cry over "the one that got away," instead of spending time building and keeping loving connections with the people in our lives now.

Yes, I know these aren't all true about everyone, but too many of us are so focused on what we're wishing for or upset about; we are ignoring and neglecting what we have!

Instead of happy, many of us end up feeling empty and dissatisfied with only a mountain of debt and a house full of junk to show for it.

If you find all this upsetting, please FORGIVE yourself or whoever else you're upset with! I'm NOT calling your attention to this way of thinking to make you feel bad! YOU ARE NOT ALONE; in the US, this way of life is NORMAL for us!

More importantly, we can't address a problem that we don't even know exists! Now that you are aware of what's really going on, you can do something about it, and today can be the beginning of a NEW WAY OF THINKING AND A NEW WAY OF LIFE!

"So, what is real happiness?"

We already know, but let me say it anyway: **Real HAPPINESS comes from giving and receiving love, and taking care of those who love and care for you.**

Sure, nice things are... nice, but they'll never love you back or care for you. Happiness is doing things for each other and doing things together! Yes, vacations are great, but everyday tasks like making dinner and cleaning house are at least as important as the trip of a lifetime!

Most kids (young kids!), who haven't already been indoctrinated with a "pursuit of happiness" mentality; would rather spend time working together, laughing together, and talking together instead of having parents who work 12 to 18 hours a day to provide them with all the nice things they really don't need.

Am I saying you should quit your job? **NO!** But we all need to think about what's really important to us, so we can create a good balance in our lives!

Family Time

What if doing yard work, cleaning house, and washing and detailing cars with your parents or kids could actually be FUN instead of a battle?

What if being in the kitchen making dinner TOGETHER, laughing, eating, and even cleaning together could become a team effort and an act of love?

Cool, huh?

If the thought of your family doing housework and cooking as a happy team seems a little strange, even outright ridiculous, GREAT! It's okay to feel however you feel, but believe it or not, it is very possible! Change doesn't happen overnight, but it can happen if you're willing to keep learning!

Just imagine how different all our lives would be if we learned to see and treat each other as beloved blessings instead of aggravating burdens? I hope you're at least curious enough to keep reading and find out how!

We're going to go through a step by step process that will put you firmly on the road to a happy life. I'm going to give you simple, easy, small habits to create that will help you learn to think differently on purpose.

Some of the things I say may seem overly simple and obvious, but they're all important! Follow the steps and do what I ask you to do and you will notice changes in yourself and the people around you!

Alright, let's get started!

It's time to CREATE HAPPINESS instead of pursuing it!

"Success is getting and achieving what you want. Happiness is wanting and being content with what you get."

-Bernard Meltzer

Chapter 4 Love What You Have

"What? No kidding! Everybody knows that!"

True! But we don't live that way!

Most of us don't think very often about all the good things in our lives! We just take them for granted because we're so used to things being the way they are. We think we're ALWAYS going to have those parents, grandparents, or kids. We feel like we're STUCK with that family, school, job, home or car, but nothing is guaranteed!

Here's a better way to think and act!

Key to HAPPINESS 1: LOVE WHAT YOU HAVE

(Sound a little cheesy and cliché to you, too? That's okay!)

I'm going to ask you write down lists of what's important to you. To me, writing is just thinking on paper! It allows you to think through things in an organized way that you can't do inside your head, so it's very beneficial for high school students as well as senior citizens! Like I say in the classroom, "humor the crazy man and just do what I ask you to do!"

Keep in mind, this is NOT going to be graded or critiqued! It's just a list for you, so don't worry about trying to be perfect!

Let's do this! What are the things that are good in your life?

Yes, what you have may not be perfect, probably not exactly what you want, but a job that pays the bills is better than no job! A car that gets you from point A to point B, and a home that keeps you dry when it rains are more than what many people have! Follow the prompts below and write about the good things in your life!

Reflection 1: WHAT ARE THE THINGS YOU ARE GRATEFUL FOR IN YOUR LIFE?

Job/Career and things at work/school	What's good about them?
Home/Car/Possessions	What's good about them?

Done? GREAT! This list is important because these are some reasons why you are/could/should be HAPPY RIGHT NOW! So dog ear or bookmark these pages! Even if you're like most of us and don't feel happy every moment of the day, these are good reasons why your life is fine, and you should be grateful and happy!

Now let's focus on people! Of course your family and friends can be annoying, but if you were going to be really honest, who are the people you're grateful for? Here's a list to fill out. BE HONEST! No one has to see this but you!

Reflection 2: WHO ARE THE PEOPLE YOU ARE GRATEFUL FOR IN YOUR LIFE?

Family Members	Why you're grateful
Friends/Coworkers	Why you're grateful
Other people? Teacher? Mailman? Good Neighbor? Cashier at a store?	Why you're grateful

If you need more room, GOOD! Continue on a piece of paper.

Did you get it done? **EXCELLENT! You ROCK!** Now that you've thought it through, it's time to put this new awareness into action!

The most important thing to remember when starting a new habit is to START SMALL! Big changes only last as long as they're NEW and EXCITING! That's why we're usually more successful when we first try to lose weight, or start an exercise program. New is fun, but sadly it's short lived.

Small changes are easy to maintain even when we're not EXCITED! We can continue them even if we're not in a good mood and sometimes they can even change our mood for the better! There'll be more info about that soon!

For now, it's time to start our first **HABIT FOR HAPPINESS**

HABIT FOR HAPPINESS 1:

Have an ATTITUDE OF GRATTITUDE!

Say "thank you!" do something nice, or pay a compliment to someone in your life **at least once a day!** It can be someone on your list, someone else you forgot, or even someone you've never met before.

Tell someone important how much he or she means to you! You could say something like, *"yes, I do get upset with you sometimes, but I hope you know how much I love you and how blessed I am to have you in my life! Thank you for all you do for us/me."* Then finish with a hug.

21

Be ready for some tears! People are usually shocked by such demonstrations of love and kindness!

If that's not the way your relationships work, you can be the one to start a change for the better!

But for now, you can start small!

-Say "Thank you for… (dinner, all the work you do, our home, the rides to school, etc…)"
-Say "What can I help you with?" if you see someone cleaning, cooking, mowing, etc… and then HELP!
-Send a text or email, or even post on someone's wall on social media! (#gratitude)

Of course, you don't have to! If just the thought of saying or doing that with some of your friends and family members makes you feel awkward and uncomfortable, and you'd rather call or text and ask how they're doing, that's okay, too! YOU'RE A GOOD PERSON and you'll decide what's best for you! It's up to you what act of kindness you will do daily! JUST DO SOMETHING NICE OR SAY SOMETHING NICE AT LEAST ONCE A DAY!

Small, new habits can GROW into a new way of life! A NEW NORMAL! This is the first of several habits that will deeply affect your thinking, productivity, and relationships in a very positive way. And more importantly, they will start to build in you a sense of your own goodness! By acting on this HABIT FOR HAPPINESS at LEAST ONCE A DAY, you will start to move in the direction of happiness and success.

Alrighty, it's time to commit to your first HABIT FOR HAPPINESS: Done daily it will change your thinking and help you create a **NEW NORMAL!**

Purposeful Positivity Habit for Happiness 1:
<u>An Attitude of Gratitude</u>

I, _____ , commit to being grateful and kind **ON PURPOSE** AT LEAST ONCE A DAY, so my actions will teach me to see myself as a GOOD PERSON and think positively. Every Day I will honor my commitment and say, "thank you," do something nice, or say something kind to or for someone NO MATTER HOW I FEEL. I can always do more, but I will not do less!

Signed: _____ Dated: _____

The great thing about small habits is they're easy to keep up, even when you're short on time or in a bad mood. Doing your mandatory one can and often will lead to doing much more, **but you NEVER HAVE TO!**

Have a smart phone handy? Take a picture and upload it to social media, #gratitude

If you filled out the lists and the commitment form, you probably feel better already! If you didn't do it, you can always go back and get it done now. TAKE CARE OF IT! You'll be glad you did!

BRUTAL KINDNESS Q&A:

Q-"I haven't filled out your stupid lists and commitment forms and I'm not going to! What are you going to do about it?"

A-**LOL! Nothing!** This is your life and your book, so it's up to you, but I'd think about it before I decided to not do them! If you're willing to read, why not take one more step and do this one extra thing that will help you start to live a better life?

Maybe you see yourself as too proud or too stubborn. I say GET OVER IT! Let your mind think whatever it wants to think, and then ACT RIGHT and do it anyway! Remember, you're doing this for YOU and the people in your life! Take that first step and the rest gets easier.

Q-"Yeah, but, what if all this doesn't work? What if I do this and I still don't FEEL happy?"

A-**No, you will NOT <u>FEEL</u> happy every minute of the day.** SO WHAT? NOBODY FEELS HAPPY ALL THE TIME, and thinking we SHOULD is a big part of what keeps us from feeling happy more often.

Q-"Huh? Did you just say WANTING to feel happy keeps me from actually feeling happy?"

A-**Yep! I sure did!** Turn to the next chapter to find out why!

"You cannot make yourself feel something you do not feel, but you can make yourself do right in spite of your feelings."

-Pearl S. Buck

Chapter 5 About Emotions

We've been taught to see our emotions as either good or bad. Of course it's good to feel happy, to laugh, to be in love, but that's only half of who we are!

Here's another **BIG LIE** MOST OF US KNOW isn't true, but many of us act like it should be!

We should be HAPPY all the time!

Yes, we all know that's not realistic, but many of us don't stop and think about it. If you already feel bad, worrying that there's something wrong with you because you're not happy only makes you feel WORSE! Feeling bad about feeling bad can easily become a downward spiral and nobody needs an extra burden like that!

Here's the real truth:

KEY TO HAPPINESS 2: ALL EMOTIONS HAVE THEIR PLACE and BELONG!

Sometimes it's appropriate to be angry! Anger can make you stand up against injustice, stop people from hurting you or others, fight off attackers.

About Emotions

Sometimes it's appropriate to be sad, worried, or afraid. People we love die and we're sad, friends are high or drunk and we should be afraid to let them drive home. People are doing bad and stupid things and we should be angry and worried about the consequences!

And, yes, it's okay to feel attracted to someone in a sexual way! Without sexual desire the human race would soon die out!

SO GO AHEAD AND FEEL HOW YOU FEEL!

Happy, sad, angry, afraid, and lustful are all perfectly valid and good ways to feel!

No, that does <u>NOT</u> mean we should ACT on all of our emotions, but instead of feeling ashamed or getting more upset over the fact that we feel the way we feel, we should just accept it!

We humans live on emotional roller coasters! Our feelings will change like the weather in Texas, and at times YOU, ME AND EVERYONE IS GOING TO FEEL BAD! It's okay! Accept it, work through it, and it will pass. Getting upset about how you feel will make as much of a difference as getting upset because it's raining! The rain will fall until it stops regardless of how mad or sad you get!

Also, keep in mind that ALL EMOTIONS ARE SOURCES OF ENERGY!

I know it may sound crazy right now, but you can use feelings of anger, fear, or sadness to get things done! Some of my best writing has happened when I'm sad! I'm my most productive when I'm mad or afraid!

26

Remember, whatever emotion you have RIGHT NOW, positive or negative, will pass when it passes! So why worry about it? **ACCEPT IT AND GET BACK TO WORK!**

One of the best things you can do while your emotions are raging is keep going! Acknowledge whatever you're feeling and keep doing the work!

KEEP ACTING RIGHT while you feel WRONG and you will find your negative emotions pass MUCH QUICKER! It's when we let our emotions shut us down and make us give up that we feel worse.

Ready to give your mind a focus that will help you continue to grow and be successful while still being connected to your family and friends?

Alrighty then, here we go!

"We are not here to curse the darkness, but to light the candle that can guide us thru that darkness to a safe and sane future."

-John F. Kennedy

Chapter 6 — FUTURE FOCUSED

What do you want your life to look like ten years from now? This has nothing to do with finding happiness: you've got plenty to be happy about <u>NOW</u>, but it is human nature to want things!

Wouldn't it be so much better to **BE HAPPY** with your family and friends while you work towards your goals instead of just doing the same old thing the same way over and over again?

Yes, I agree!

Humans always seem to want to be doing something. Even if it's just playing video games or being on social media, so why fight it? Let's give ourselves something to focus on! A goal to work towards!

So, what do you **WANT**? What is a future that's worth working for?

I want you to picture yourself in ten years. If you're 17, that means you'll be looking ahead to what your life will be like when you're 27. If you're 43, then what will your life be like when you're 53?

Just picture it as clearly as you can and write down what you imagine. Give as many details as possible! It doesn't have to be outrageous and pie in the sky!

Not sure how to do it right? That's okay! Do it WRONG! This is brainstorming or rough draft writing! When you're just thinking through a topic, spelling and punctuation DON'T MATTER! All that's important is that you are thinking and writing from the heart. This is for you and no one else, so FORGIVE YOURSELF for not being perfect and just do the best you can! YOU'RE A GOOD PERSON! I'm sure your best is more than good enough!

Goal Setting 1: ME TEN YEARS FROM NOW

Ten years from now I will be _____ years old.

Tell about relationships: will you be married? Single? Dating? Will you have children? More children? If yes to kids (especially if you're already a parent), how many and what ages will they be ten years from now and what will they be like?
Ten years from now I will be...

Tell about your home: (Apartment, house, or some other? How many bedrooms and bathrooms, etc...? What kind of kitchen, floors, siding, yard, etc...? Explain and give as many details as you can imagine!

Ten years from now I will be living in ...

Tell about your Career/Education/Job: In ten years, what will you be doing to make money? Describe where you think you'll be working, what you'll be doing, how much money you'll be making and what your life will be like at work. *Not sure about a career? Just pick a future that sounds good to you! This is NOT set in stone! Just take your best guess. You can also try the career and aptitude test at* https://www.psychologytoday.com/us/tests/career/career-personality-aptitude-test

Ten years from now I will be a/an...

Tell about your vehicle/transportation: how will you get around? Would you prefer a car? Truck? SUV? Motorcycle or scooter? Something else? Don't worry about what cars will be like in ten years! Just write about what you'd prefer now for yourself in 10 years! What color interior and exterior? What engine? What options/upgrades? Give as many details as possible!
Ten years from now I will drive...

You're DONE? You ROCK!

BOTTOM LINE: Knowing what you want makes it much easier to be FUTURE FOCUSED! Remember, YOU ALREADY HAVE PLENTY TO BE HAPPY ABOUT! You already have a GOOD LIFE! If you're not feeling it yet, that's okay! We're doing this so we have a deeper understanding of what's really important to us!

Remember, being FUTURE FOCUSED doesn't mean you'll be happy when you have enough stuff or have attained a high enough level of success. We're not going to waste our time postponing happiness! The time to be happy is **NOW**! Being HAPPY AND FUTURE FOCUSED means...

-you're giving your natural, human desire for improvement a proper focus.

-You'll do more, work harder, and have a better attitude because you can clearly see what you're trying to accomplish.

-you'll push yourself because you know what you want and you're willing to work for it.

It's also easier to overlook the day to day complaints and annoyances we all have to deal with, because we're focused on what we're trying to accomplish instead of just the daily issues we ALL struggle with.

Put another way, it means "your eye is on the prize!"

Being FUTURE FOCUSED means you're working because YOU WANT TO, not because you have to! No, it doesn't mean you'll love every minute of every day at work, but living focused on the future can make a tremendous difference in your attitude and productivity. Many of us never experience the JOY OF WORK because we feel obligated, trapped, and even enslaved by our responsibilities.

BRUTAL KINDNESS Q&A:

Q-"Hold on! Did you put "joy," and "work," together in the same sentence? That must be a mistake!"

A -**NOPE! It's not!** Too many of us only see work as a necessary evil. We work because we need money, we want to buy things, and we want to spend money, but NOT because we enjoy it!

We DON'T think work is good and makes us better people. No, most of us work because we're afraid of the consequences of not working! So we DRAG through our day feeling miserable and bored because we are doing as little as possible.

Q-*"Well, what if I almost NEVER feel motivated? What if I just hate doing work?"*

A-That means you're just like I was! I felt like I was always being pushed to do things I didn't really want to do, and the more I was pushed, the less I wanted to do whatever needed to get done.

The quickest way to kill motivation and enthusiasm is to say, "You HAVE TO!" or, "Get it done, OR ELSE!" But parents, teachers, and bosses default to those kinds of tactics all too often!

And guess what? They work just well enough to keep everything moving but make NOBODY HAPPY! The workers feel like their boss treats them like sled dogs who need to hear the crack of a whip; and the bosses watches those workers like a hawk because they think they will only work if someone is pushing or making them.

Sound familiar? It's because that's how most things get done these days!

We need to understand that fear of consequences will only motivate you to do enough to avoid punishment, avoid getting fired, or avoid getting yelled at or hit, but it will almost never motivate you to do your best; being FUTURE FOCUSED WILL!

Being FUTURE FOCUSED is the difference between, "I HAVE TO PASS or my parents will TAKE MY PHONE AWAY," and "I WANT to be an entrepreneur and start my own business, so I'm going to WORK MY HARDEST and DO MY BEST to learn all I can!"

When you're FUTURE FOCUSED, you are working for you and you're working with PASSION because you can already see what you're trying to accomplish. Believe it or not, you might start to **ENJOY WORK!**

Q –yeah, but what if my boss is just a jerk?

A -We've all had a bad boss, or a bad teacher! Instead of focusing on arguing or trying to get out of doing the work you know you're supposed to do, you'll be thinking about the career and FUTURE you created for yourself, and have that much more reason to work through those difficulties instead of getting frustrated, mad, and giving up.

YOU ARE A GOOD PERSON! If you didn't do the writing a few pages back, I do it now. If you did do the writing as requested, look back over what you wrote before, and on the next page write down the specific things you're planning for the future without all the details: **You can also fill this in even if you haven't done and don't plan on doing the previous writing.** Especially for those of us who are **LAZY**, this one is much less work, so just do it!

Goal Setting 2: The FUTURE I'm Working For

Career	
Education/training	
Relationships	
Home	
Vehicle	

Post your future on social media with #FutureFocused

Done? You ROCK! Having these goals clear in your mind is POWERFUL! No, you probably won't be focused on them for every moment of the day, but they can, and often do, pull you in the right direction!

In fact, let's make this into another easy, small habit. Fill out the form on the next page, please!

Purposeful Positivity HABIT FOR HAPPINESS 2:

Being **FUTURE FOCUSED**

I, _____, commit to

checking in on my goals/future AT LEAST once a day, so I keep moving, working, and doing my best to live into the future I created. Every Day I will honor my commitment NO MATTER HOW I FEEL. I can always do more, but I will not do less!

Signed: _____ Dated: _____

WOO HOO! You rock! Once a day, think about what your goals are and what you're trying to accomplish.

"I'm lazy. But it's the lazy people who invented the wheel and the bicycle because they didn't like walking or carrying things."

-Lech Walesa

Chapter 7 ...But, I'm LAZY!"

Who's lazy? You, me, and, in my opinion, about 90% of us!

I read somewhere that 10 or 15% of us do 90% of the work. I also remember reading *Atlas Shrugged* by Ayn Rand, in which the very few at the top of the most ambitious and successful people decide to "drop" the weight of the world and let all the lazy and stupid people fall on their faces and maybe even die.

That'll teach 'em, right!?

Well... no... not really.

Here's another **BIG LIE** that most of us believe to be true: **Lazy people need to be taught a lesson!**

Lazy kids are really my favorite! They're the ones who usually have no idea how smart they are and no idea why they're so lazy. They usually think it's because there's something wrong, some character flaw that keeps them from getting things done. Often, when I ask why they're not doing their work, I get a shrug and then I hear the words, "I dunno...I guess I'm just lazy...."

It always FREAKS them out when I smile at them and laugh! I'm laughing because I know exactly how they feel! They're just like I was! Here's the TRUTH that I didn't know then, but has made a HUGE difference in my life now:

Lazy kids aren't really lazy; THEY'RE REBELLIOUS!

Like I said before, many believe lazy people need some form of punishment or discipline, but the lessons we try to teach only reinforce what most of us lazy people already think we know; **YOU'RE MEAN, SO I DON'T WANT TO WORK FOR YOU!**

How is punishing someone going to change that belief?

Right, it won't! It just reinforces it! No amount of punishment will ever change a lazy person's thinking, but learning what's taught in this book can!

Rather than explaining more, let me show you. I think my story is pretty typical of a lazy teenager. I was so tired of being pushed around by my father and made to feel like nothing I ever did was good enough, that somewhere along the way I decided that I wasn't going to try anymore.

Dad was ALWAYS MAD, or at least he seemed that way. If I didn't do what I was told, I was going to at least get yelled at and maybe even hit; so just saying "no!" was pretty much out of the question.

Instead of trying to fight with a bigger, stronger, grown man, I did the opposite: I quit trying! I went out of my way to NOT do what he wanted without ever actually saying, "no!"

Steve versus Dad

Now when you're young and have a tough parent, you feel mistreated and pushed around; Instead of trying to fight directly, you fight indirectly! **You DRAG! When it came to DRAGGING, I was a pro!**

(I act this scene out for my classes every year!)

I was a tall, skinny 13 or 14-year-old and Dad was a short, stern, gray haired, 60-year-old man with glasses. Just about every weekend Dad got tired of seeing me lie around, so he decided I needed to clean the bathroom, mow, pull weeds, or rake leaves.

He'd walked up to me like he was a drill sergeant and I was a new recruit who just showed up for boot camp. **"Now you listen! You get the rake and get to the back yard! Those leaves are piling up and you BETTER take care of it! NOW!"**

Of course, I whined! "Awww MAN! Are you serious! I was gonna watch TV!"

Dad was an old, racist, angry Hispanic man and he hated when I used the word, "man" like that because he said I was trying to sound "black!" So, of course, I used it every chance I got!

"Don't talk like that!" he'd say. "You get out there NOW and you GET TO WORK!"

Did I rush to do my father's bidding? Did I say, "Yessir!" jump right up and attack that pile of leaves?

Of course not! Instead **I DRAGGED!**

I got up slowly, sighing, complaining under my breath, and making noises of misery and servitude! "Ugh…. I HATE raking leaves. This is SO stupid."

Dad glared and his voice had a sharp edge to it, **"WHAT DID YOU SAY?"**

"Nothing!" I snapped. "Why you always mad for?"

Dad wasn't having it! **"HURRY UP or I'll give you something to complain about!"**

I pretended to walk faster; if you raise your elbows and knees a little higher and move your arms a little quicker, that's usually enough to keep you from getting smacked without actually moving any faster in the direction you don't want to go!

 Finally I retrieved the rake and trash bags from the carport and DRAGGED my way to the back yard. Once there, I attacked my task with all the vigor of a sloth that had just eaten a full meal.

Dad soon came by to see if I was working. Of course, I heard him coming, so I sped up! I was doing just enough to keep from getting hit, but not enough to keep from getting yelled at.

"Why are you moving so SLOW? HURRY UP! Look! You do it like THIS!" He grabbed the rake out of my nearly still hands with the speed of a cobra striking, and proceeded to show me how it was done.

With a great flurry, he attacked the leaves, kicking up clouds of dust and doing more work in 30 seconds than I'd done in half an hour. Then he threw the rake back at me, and the sound of a cracking whip was in his voice. **"There! Now GET TO WORK!"** The rake handle bounced off my shoulder, but I somehow caught it before it fell to the ground.

I was actually kinda scared…. I thought I SHOULD just get to work…. Instead, **I DRAGGED SOME MORE!** I whined, "This is SOOOOO STUPID! I hate raking leaves! Why do I have to do this?"

"HURRY UP, GODDAMN IT!" he yelled, and raised his hand like he was going to hit me.

"Okay, okay," I'd say and move my arms a little faster, but then I soon went back to dragging. I went slower… and slower….

He'd fuss and yell, maybe even smack me with a stinging swat on my arm or leg, which only made me work faster for about 30 seconds, but then I'd whine and complain even more. This could go on for HOURS!

Every now and then we would keep on like this until I FINALLY got it done, but most of the time he just wasn't that patient. Most of the time he'd eventually get fed up with me!

He'd scream, **"I CAN'T STAND YOU! You're so goddamned LAZY! JUST GET OUT OF HERE!"**

41

I looked and acted hurt and shocked as I walked away with tears in my eyes; but once I was far enough away that he couldn't see my face, I was SMILING, and I wanted to LAUGH!

I knew better than to actually do that! You can't act happy, because then he'd realize he'd been tricked, and he'd be right back on you like gum on your shoe!

In the war to make me work, it was Steve 1 and Dad 0!

YES! HAHA! I got away with not doing what I was told, and I ENJOYED the WIN!

The problem was that he wasn't the only one being tricked!

I was tricking myself! My ACTIONS were proof that I was a...

- lazy
- miserable
- weak
- liar

Keep in mind; I never consciously thought this about myself! I just knew I hated my Dad because he was mean, and the rest just... happened. Those responses to authority became automatic with repeated practice, so pretty soon it was just the way I felt and the way I was.

Since Dad regularly screamed himself hoarse telling me how lazy, useless, and no good I was whenever he tried to make me work, and I never stopped to think about it, I swallowed those beliefs as truths.

Those beliefs didn't just affect me with Dad! I spent a lot of years reinforcing them—DRAGGING in school or at work—or fighting them—pulling all night study sessions before a test, or staying late at work to get things finished after I fell behind—but I never questioned the actual beliefs until much later because I didn't know they were beliefs. I didn't think I was ACTING any way: It was just the way I was and the way things were.

Our behavior and CONDITIONING

If you know you're lazy and **DRAG**, or you get **MAD** and **PUNISH** and **PUSH**, you've had years of conditioning, too! Actually, we all have!

Most of us have heard of Pavlov's dog; a scientist would ring a bell every time he was about to give a dog food, so that eventually all he had to do was ring the bell and the dog would salivate. It required no thought on the dog's part: it was on AUTOPILOT!

It's the same with us! We've each been trained to act the way we do by a LIFETIME of CONDITIONING! We grow up with adults in charge who push and punish because that's how they were raised, and we DRAG because nobody likes to be pushed around and feel like you don't have a choice; but when we're the ones in charge, we'll probably push and punish, too!

The really difficult thing to understand is that even after that parent, or other authority figure from your childhood is no longer in your daily life, your beliefs about authority are probably now part of your character.

So, even as an adult, all somebody has to do is talk to you with an authoritative voice, fuss and complain, or make threats, and it will engage your **DRAG Reflex**—Get it? Like gag reflex; it's a pun! —and we're suddenly on AUTOPILOT and not doing what we KNOW we're supposed to do!

You're not doing it on purpose, but you are most likely not doing as good as you could! MOST OF US HAVE BEEN CONDITIONED TO DO LESS THAN OUR BEST, BUT WE DON'T HAVE TO STAY THAT WAY!

Here's another important point; if you are habitually talking to yourself like an angry parent or coach, you are probably DRAGGING in response to yourself, too! The best thing we can do is talk back to the "have to," mindset! Realize YOU DON'T HAVE TO DO ANYTHING!

The best daily conversation you can have with yourself is "what do I want? What do I REALLY want?" (Right! Take a moment every day and do your 2nd Habit for Happiness, so you'll be #FutureFocused)

Keep in mind; it should be no surprise that neither you nor your parents are perfect! Your parents did the best they could and so did you! Instead of wasting energy blaming anyone, it's a good time to start letting that go and start working for a better future! **FORGIVE** and remind yourself:

I DON'T HAVE TO BE LAZY! I CAN DO ANYTHING I WANT!

Let's write about it. Like I've said before, writing is really thinking on paper and it's the best way to think because it gets your thoughts organized and out of your head. As usual, spelling and punctuation DON'T MATTER! This is rough draft writing and it's your thoughts that matter and should be the focus, NOT spelling or punctuation!

Reflection 3: DRAGGING

What does DRAGGING look like for you? Do you get distracted? Do you argue and fuss? Do you get nervous, sad, or mad? Explain and give details!
What situations usually engage your DRAG REFLEX? At school/work and at home, when do you usually find yourself putting things off or skipping things you know you should do? Explain and give details.
What's really important? ("Me 10 years From Now.")

EXCELLENT! Glad you got it done!

We have already learned a lot! Before we move on to the next chapter and how to apply this information on DRAGGING, let's recap:

1. **HAPPINESS COMES FROM GIVING AND RECEIVING LOVE, NOT FROM THINGS! <u>IT CAN'T BE PURSUED!</u>** Trying to find happiness in new experiences, new toys, or circumstances, means you're only wasting your time and growing more distant from the people in your life! NOW IS THE BEST TIME TO BE HAPPY AND THANKFUL! Remember to honor your commitment and compliment someone, say "thank you," or be kind AT LEAST once a day.

2. **ALL EMOTIONS HAVE THEIR PLACE AND BELONG! Thinking we should BE HAPPY ALL THE TIME IS NOT REALISTIC-** Emotions aren't good or bad! They just are! Learn to accept how you feel, and you'll find the times when you feel bad or down pass much more quickly!

3. **HAVING GOALS FOR THE FUTURE MAKES IT EASIER TO DO YOUR BEST IN THE PRESENT-** It means you're working to get what you want for your life, so it's easier to work harder and do better! Honor your commitment and check in on your goals EVERY DAY!

4. **YOU'RE PROBABLY NOT LAZY; YOU'RE REBELLIOUS!** Most of us are DRAGGING and doing less than our best! Learning to recognize when you're DRAGGING means you now KNOW you can

do something different and work HARD to get what YOU want!

5. **WE'RE ALL PRODUCTS OF CONDITIONING!** You probably don't even realize what you're doing or how you're acting because you've been trained to be this way your whole life! Following the steps in this book is the only thing that has allowed me to break away from the past!

Alrighty then! These five concepts put into practice are already enough to change your life for the better!

Remember, this is groundwork to set you up for the **REALLY POWERFUL ones**! Be **BRUTALLY KIND** to yourself and be ready to move forward and do the work!

BRUTAL KINDNESS:

You can just nod and say, "Yeah, you're right! I'm not going to act that way anymore!" but then old habits will return, and you'll be back on autopilot! Instead, it's time to learn a better way to live. It's time to learn how to ACT on these truths instead of just thinking about them! But first, think about all you've written about, and all you want for the future.

You do want better for yourself, right?
Why else would you have even picked up this book?
Turn the page and let's get to work!

"You gotta do it with class and integrity. If not, you're gonna drag yourself through the mud."

-Solomon Burke

Chapter 8   Living with Integrity

What if you decided to ACT RIGHT ALL THE TIME? I'm not just talking about when you're at a job interview or when you meet someone important, but ALL DAY EVERY DAY! How would that affect you and your life?

Think about it: What if you ALWAYS did your homework, met your deadlines, ate right and exercised, got to work or school on time, and even always said please and thank you? How would your life be different? How differently would others see you?

We're going to do our best to find out!

It's time to take our feelings out of the driver's seat and move them to the back seat where they belong. It's time to focus on INTEGRITY!

INTEGRITY means you DO WHAT'S RIGHT NO MATTER HOW YOU FEEL.

Forget about putting on a show. Don't waste time pointing out that other people might act much worse than you do and focus on YOUR ACTIONS.

In a moment, I'm going to ask you to think about the way you've acted and the dishonest things you've done. Don't worry; nobody is looking to punish you! This is just to wake you up and make you aware of how often you take shortcuts instead of doing what's right. **Remember, recognizing your mistakes is the first step to doing something about them! Your whole life has conditioned you to act this way! But don't worry! Regardless of the past, you can still have a GREAT present and future!**

If you start getting upset or feeling guilty, **FORGIVE YOURSELF** as many times as you have to! Nobody has to know what you've done in the past but you! I'm also purposely NOT going to ask you to make a list or write about it! I don't want someone to find this later and use it as an excuse to get mad at you!

You may think, "I DON'T STEAL! BUT… "

- one day you saw someone leave behind a smart phone, ear buds, or money; and instead of giving them back, you kept whatever it was. Maybe you used someone else's account to buy things without them knowing it.

-At work or school, you've eaten food or drank drinks you didn't pay for, made personal copies on the company copy machine, or took home paper, pens, and/or paperclips. You borrowed things you never returned. You've zone out, or struck up a conversation with a coworker or friend and wasted time when you knew you had work to do.

-You were really broke, so you kept the extra change the cashier gave you by accident, or the cash in a wallet you found.

You might think, "I DON'T LIE!" BUT…

-You've called in sick to work or missed school because you were too stressed out, hung over, or just wanted a day off to lie around and play.

-You told your friend or coworker that you have other plans when you really just didn't feel like hanging out with him or her.

-You've had one or more affairs or hook ups (online or in person) and lied about it. You looked up content online that you're ashamed of and don't want ANYONE to find out about.

-You lied to hurt someone you don't like, or to protect someone you love.

Here's the <u>BRUTAL</u> truth:

The more shortcuts we take with our INTEGRITY, the more it affects us behind the scenes. The more we let little lies and petty thefts become the norm, the more it hurts our self-images and erodes our self-respect.

BRUTAL KINDNESS:

Okay, that list is DONE! Whew! Don't waste any energy on feeling BAD!

Feeling BAD does no GOOD! **YOU'RE A GOOD PERSON** even if you don't always feel like it! That's why you're reading this right now!

FEELING GUILTY DOESN'T HELP, but learning to change the way you ACT, so your future is different from your past, can and will make a HUGE DIFFERENCE! It has for me!

Here's a truth that will help you change your focus.

KEY TO HAPPINESS 3: What you DO is what REALLY matters!

WHAT YOU DO, NOT WHAT YOU THINK OR FEEL defines you! ACTIONS will always speak louder than words, and MUCH LOUDER than thoughts!

BRUTAL KINDNESS:
If your mind is disagreeing with me right now, Oh well! LET IT! THE TRUTH IS THOUGHTS ARE MEANINGLESS UNLESS THEY ARE ACTED UPON! If you stop and think about it, you'll know I'm right.

Q -"So, how do I do that? How do I NOT focus on my thoughts and emotions?"

A -First, accept the fact that you and I will probably ALWAYS have bad thoughts; our emotions will still push us to do things that aren't good for us no matter how hard we try or want things to be different. Like I said before, the weather is not going to change just because we want it to! **Then, it's time to get over it!** Let it go like a helium balloon! It's time to FOCUS ON OUR ACTIONS, because those are the only things you REALLY CAN control!

The only way that I've ever found that helps people change their negative thinking to positive is for people to start ACTING like ... "I'M A GOOD PERSON! I DO WHAT'S RIGHT NO MATTER HOW I FEEL!"

If you're ACTING RIGHT, what you feel or think DOESN'T MATTER! SERIOUSLY!

-You can be so filled with envy or greed, that you **REALLY** want to steal that brand new, shiny smart phone or wallet full of cash; but if you never actually do it, **you are guilty of no crime and the police will not come looking for you.**

-You can **HATE** someone and want to **KILL** that person for years, and as long as you don't do it, **you are not a murderer!**

-You can **lust after** and want to **tackle** and **have sex** with someone literally every day, but as long as you don't actually do it, you haven't hurt anyone and **you're not a rapist!**

So, why think less of yourself for having bad thoughts?

I say it's time to learn how to BE PROUD OF YOURSELF for NOT acting on them!

YES! BE PROUD OF YOURSELF FOR DOING WHAT'S RIGHT NO MATTER HOW YOU FEEL!

The problem is that because of our conditioning, your old habits (right, AUTOPILOT!) are not going to just change! YOU HAVE TO DO IT ON PURPOSE!

That means you start living with INTEGRITY as your guide, NOT your emotions!

"Amateurs wait for inspiration. The real pros get up and go to work."

-Harvey Mackay

Chapter 9: Integrity In Action

When we're sad or mad, angry or frustrated, it's all too easy to take shortcuts. Especially if you're like me and you've been living this way basically all of your life! Our emotions can and do hijack us and, before we know it, we've engaged our **DRAG REFLEX**, or done something else dishonest, sneaky, or mean!

BRUTAL KINDNESS:

So, when you're in a bad mood and you feel like you really have no choice but to fall back into old bad habits, **there's only one way to continue to live in INTEGRITY...**

S U F F E R !

And DO WHAT'S RIGHT NO MATTER HOW YOU FEEL!

In our society, we tend to see SUFFERING as a bad thing that we should avoid, but I disagree!

Now, I DON'T literally mean to seek out abuse, or torture yourself!

Not at all!

I mean have the **INTEGRITY** to **ACT RIGHT!** Persist in doing the right thing no matter what your subconscious mind and emotions throw at you!

SUFFERING through your emotions helps you realize that what you feel isn't the truth! You can feel CRAZY, ANGRY, SCARED and still...

-WORK through your bad moods!

-KEEP GOING when you want to quit!

-STEP OUT OF YOUR COMFORT ZONE and try something new!

-HONOR THAT COMMITMENT even though you're tired, grumpy and regret having said, "Yes, I'll be there."

Every time you SUFFER and ACT RIGHT while you still feel wrong, you prove to yourself that you are A GOOD PERSON!

And, MOST IMPORTANTLY, you'll feel GOOD ABOUT YOURSELF FOR GETTING THINGS DONE, instead of feeling bad because you have bad thoughts or didn't do what you knew you were supposed to do!

You may have to be **BRUTALLY KIND** to do it, but if you keep doing what's right during the times you'd rather just take a shortcut, you'll start changing how you see yourself as well as how the world sees you!

Like I said before, the real you is who you are in the world! Your actions based on INTEGRITY will begin to reset your AUTOPILOT! You will rebuild your self-image and over time your ACTIONS will teach you that YOU ARE A GOOD PERSON, but only if you learn how to **SUFFER!**

S U F F E R I N G FOR SUCCESS

Here's how it works:

Feel however you feel and think whatever you think, and then be **BRUTALLY KIND** enough to be TOUGH ON YOURSELF! SMILE (yes, a FAKE smile is better than no smile!), SUFFER and GET TO WORK!

The SMILE is important because it tells your mind you're just fine, and somehow the SMILING, and the doing together changes the way we feel and think way faster than doing either of those things separately!

The more often you ACT RIGHT no matter how you feel the quicker it will become a new habit, a NEW NORMAL!

PURPOSEFUL POSITIVITY MEANS YOU CHOOSE to have INTEGRITY, so you SMILE, SUFFER and...

- Instead of lying because it's easier, tell the truth!
- Instead of keeping the extra change the cashier gave you, hand it back so she or he doesn't get in trouble.
- Instead of yelling at your kids or getting in a fight with your parents, go cool off and then talk to them calmly about your concerns.
- If you do yell at someone because you're angry, cool off and then apologize to that person.

When you raise the INTEGRITY bar higher you will quickly see how it affects your thinking, your self-image, and self-esteem. This is easy to do on a good day, but it won't be so easy when we're tired, stressed, and in a rush! We may think things like...

"I work really hard and I'm tired, so I just CAN'T exercise, and I DESERVE to eat that whole pint of ice cream!"

Or

"My wife/husband/parents/kids ALWAYS screw up and I'm REALLY fed up! It's my family's fault I yelled at them!"

Or even,

"I've been through SO MUCH, been so STRESSED OUT that I CAN'T go to work/school today and do my job! Nobody can judge me because they DON'T UNDERSTAND what I've been through!"

When my students act that way, I've learned to be **BRUTALLY KIND,** SMILE and say, **"GOOD! SUFFER!" and usually they then get to work!**

You're NOT my student! You can be **BRUTALLY KIND** to yourself! When you SUFFER and have the INTEGRITY to SMILE and ACT productive and energetic, you are moving yourself closer to your goals and closer to success.

Most importantly, by having INTEGRITY, you are proving to yourself that YOU'RE A GOOD PERSON, AND WE ALL KNOW THAT GOOD PEOPLE DESERVE TO BE HAPPY!

SO LET THE STORMS OF YOUR MIND RAGE! If you stop and think about it, most of the fear, sadness, and anger is really your mind responding to conditioning and rebelling against a routine that isn't fun and new anymore so you'll fall back into old habits! To teach your mind a better way, all you have to do is SUFFER!

Here are some ways we can become more successful:

Get into an argument at school or at work and be MAD! Be so angry you can't think straight, and then take a deep breath, SMILE, SUFFER, and ACT CALM and in control. Keep doing your job or class work to the best of your ability; return that customer's phone call, take those notes, or reply politely and respectfully to that email even if your hands are shaking as you do it.

Find out your son wrecked his car... or your car, or you parent or spouse got fired or quit his or her job **AGAIN;** and take deep breaths, SMILE, SUFFER, and ACT CALM and clean up that mess, pick up your pencil and write that essay, smile and say "hello!" to that customer, etc....

Be stressed out and worried so much that you're literally trembling, and still have the INTEGRITY to SMILE, SUFFER and BE KIND to that annoying person you want to snap at, play a board game with your kids/siblings, do the dishes.

Like our ATTITUDE OF GRATITUDE Habit, this one starts small as well! Once a day can change your thinking LONG-TERM and that's what we're looking for! As you build INTEGRITY you will find it easier to...

SUFFER, SMILE and take out the trash.

SUFFER, SMILE and thank your spouse or parents for always taking good care of you and your home.

SUFFER, SMILE and clean up that mess right away instead of ignoring it.

The sooner you start, the sooner you will learn to see yourself as A GOOD PERSON because your actions are the proof! You will have started an UPWARD SPIRAL instead of following the old habits that lead you into a downward spiral.

You really can't understand how much more peaceful and balanced your life will become unless you experience it for yourself.

But first, you will SUFFER! Below is a little graph of what most of us would do on a NORMAL day with our emotions in charge. It shows what our actions would be like if we let our emotions be KING and tell us what to do.

An Ordinary Day with Emotions as KING!

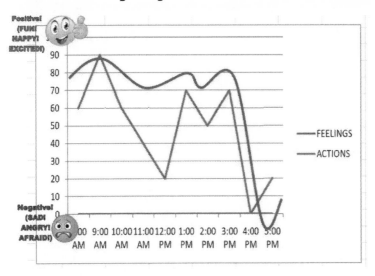

It's black and white, so it's hard to tell, but ACTIONS is the line that's mostly on top! Most of us start out pretty good, and even manage to work through a bad mood, or do some hard work, but as the day goes on and we get tired, we find ourselves **DRAGGING**, slacking, maybe even cheating or stealing because our negative emotions push us and we're used to following our feelings. If we also have arguments, break ups, financial worries, or etc… that cut into our sleep and keep us from getting rest, we could do much worse!

Below is how it would look like if we SUFFER and focus on INTEGRITY instead of following what our thoughts and feelings prompt us to do. When our emotions CRASH, SUFFERING means our ACTIONS stay positive anyway!

An Ordinary Day with INTEGRITY as KING!

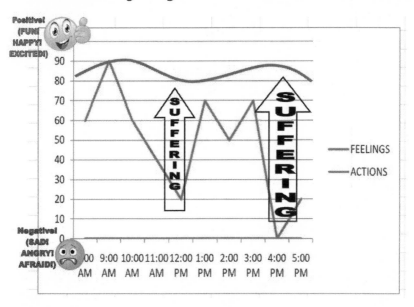

ACTING RIGHT while you feel WRONG requires SUFFERING! PERIOD! STOP! Accept it, ACT RIGHT, and life becomes much EASIER and much BETTER! Instead of focusing on how you feel and letting your emotions push you to act negatively and do poorly, you'll SUFFER and keep ACTING RIGHT!

Your emotions will go up or down as they please and yes, you probably won't do as well as you could if you felt GREAT, but you'll do far better than if you just did what your emotions nudged you to do!

Yes, you will have to SUFFER sometimes to ACT RIGHT, especially while you feel wrong, but remember;

On the other side of SUFFERING is SUCCESS!

Usually, once you're in ACTION, SUFFERING ends! Once your mind has accepted that YOU'RE GOING TO DO WHAT'S RIGHT NO MATTER HOW YOU FEEL, those emotions will back off and you will have one more reason to believe YOU ARE A GOOD PERSON, as well as a deeper understanding that our emotions are NOT the truth! **SO SUFFER!** You are SUFFERING because you care about yourself and the people around you!

Remember, SUFFERING is NOT punishment and neither is work! SUFFERING is building a muscle that many of us have never really used on purpose before, and as that muscle grows, so will your self-esteem and self-respect.

It's time to start an INTEGRITY HABIT!

Don't wait to think about it! JUMP ON IT! Fill out the form on the next page! This is not a legal contract; it's just a promise to <u>YOU</u> that <u>YOU</u> will begin moving in the right direction.

I know YOU'RE A GOOD PERSON! I don't need to try to make you! If you feel yourself starting to DRAG, REMEMBER TO SMILE, SUFFER, AND DO IT ANYWAY! :)

Habit for Happiness 3: **<u>INTEGRITY CHALLENGE</u>**

I, _____, commit to

have INTEGRITY and DO THE RIGHT THING AT LEAST once a day! No matter what kind of mood I'm in, I'm going to SUFFER! SMILE! And DO WHAT'S RIGHT NO MATTER HOW I FEEL, so my ACTIONS will teach me to see myself as a GOOD PERSON and think positively.

Signed: _____ Dated: _____

Got it done? **You ROCK!**
Have a smart phone handy? Take a picture and upload it! #integrity, #suffer, or #BrutalKindness

Take a minute right now to find your first thing to do!
Maybe there are some socks and/or shoes on the floor, or a dirty dish lying on the counter that you can take care of RIGHT NOW! Maybe there's an assignment you can finish or an email you can respond to RIGHT NOW! Maybe there are some clothes you can throw in the washing machine or fold and put away RIGHT NOW!

Pick one thing and do it RIGHT NOW, and then do more if you feel like it! Come back when you're done! Share on social media with #integrity or #suffer

So, you did it, and now you feel pretty good? Maybe you feel a little funny, weird, or even nervous? Maybe you did more and you're surprised at how easy it was to do extra? Or you didn't do anything and you're chuckling to yourself because you're not going to let some writer tell you what to do. Either way, **GREAT**!

If you did it, you probably feel better about yourself right now and you can use those feeling to help you start a powerful habit. Skim through the rest of this chapter (Q&A) and then move on to **FORGIVENESS**.

If you haven't done your first ACT of INTEGRITY yet, yes, you're probably DRAGGING and have been conditioned to rebel! This habit of NOT doing what you could or should is probably hurting you! It's time to take that first step towards letting that go! Use the index and read through the Q&A that follows as needed. Read what you need; skip the rest!

BRUTAL KINDNESS Q&A: Index

Q- "What if I don't need this?

I don't think this is really for me."

A-You're right! You don't need this! I'm **NOT** here to fix you! Your life will go on just the way it has so far, and you will be about as happy or unhappy as you've always been. People live their whole lives just doing what they do, and their lives are fine!

The real question is do you want more of the same or something different?

Are you satisfied with your current level of success and the way your relationships are with family, friends, and coworkers? If the answer is no, then this is the perfect time to get over it and get to work!

If you're normally lazy, angry, fussy, or you're used to giving up and quitting, then this is the perfect time to recognize what you're doing to yourself: YOU'RE DRAGGING YOUR WAY TO FAILURE AND QUITTING AGAIN!

Instead, SUFFER, ACT RIGHT, and LEARN TO WORK THROUGH IT!

Q-"Yeah, but it just seems dumb!

Integrity Challenge? Really? Whatever!"

A- Yes, really! Think about the way you feel right now and all the things you've quit or failed at in the past. This probably isn't the first time you've felt that way! You're probably responding to your conditioning! A lot of us don't like to do what we're told, so we get MAD! If getting MAD is a habit, it can be just as destructive as DRAGGING.

When you tend to get and stay MAD, your pride/anger/superiority pushes you to do things that are bad for you and hurt others! If you're thinking, "Ain't NOBODY gonna tell ME what to do!" or "I ain't gotta listen to you!" **You're right! You don't!**

It's time to take a deep breath! It's time to relax on purpose, because as long as we're on HIGH ALERT, it's hard to think through things clearly. Take a break if you need to and come back when you're ready....

Okay, glad you're back! When you get MAD and quit, you're hurting yourself and others and most of the time you're not even aware of it!

Do your INTEGRITY CHALLENGE Habit for the first time, and FORGIVE yourself for being prideful and stubborn. You're used to getting angry, so being aware of it and learning to react differently will help you immensely! If you're ready to make a change, a LASTING CHANGE, please go on the next chapter!

Q-"Who are you to judge me?

I'm not doing anything wrong!

I'm not acting; I'm just being me!"

A -Right! You are just being you! Whether you want to accept it or not, being you IS HOW YOU'RE ACTING! You're so conditioned by your life experiences, so used to being you that you can't... won't even see it!

But you can ACT different if you're willing to SUFFER! You're probably on autopilot right now and either MAD, DRAGGING, or both; and in the past that probably has stopped you from getting what you want out of life!

Stop and think about it and then do what's best for you! You're the only one who can decide what that is.

Remember, you're probably DRAGGING right now! I'm not trying to make you feel bad or win a battle to make you work; I'm trying to help you get what <u>YOU</u> want out of <u>YOUR</u> life!

Look back at what you want your life to be like in your "Me, Ten Years From Now" writing, and then decide what you really want to do.

The thing is, whether it's pride, anger, fear, or laziness, no amount of yelling with capital letters from me will be enough to make you do the work! You have to learn to be **BRUTALLY KIND** enough to make yourself do things because you care enough to be tough on you! Work because you want to succeed and reach your goals and create the HAPPINESS we all say we want. Nobody can do it for you!

So, just as it's always been, it's up to YOU! SMILE! You'll do the INTEGRITY CHALLENGE if or when you're ready! This book will still be here any time you change your mind and choose to DO WHAT'S RIGHT NO MATTER HOW YOU FEEL.

Q-"What if I've already screwed up too much?

I'm afraid it's not gonna help."

A- You're too hard on yourself! A lot of us just don't know how to let go of past mistakes and end up using our failures as excuses to not even try. But even if inside you REALLY think you're no good, you can still SUFFER and take a leap of faith; take this first step to create a new way of thinking and living!

Let's be realistic here: NOBODY does everything right all the time. **NOBODY!**

If you're thinking you can't do it, what you mean is, you can't do it PERFECTLY. You're probably right! And to that I say, **SO WHAT!**

I've been living in INTEGRITY for YEARS and I still mess up regularly! CONDITIONING DOESN'T GO AWAY! If you're doing the best you can, then that's all anyone can ask.

Trying to DO WHAT'S RIGHT NO MATTER HOW I FEEL means I get it right about 85-90% of the time! That's way better than my old normal way of about 45-50% and it's well enough for other people and for me to have a much different perception of the kind of person I am.

The same can be true for you! FORGIVE yourself for not being perfect and do the work!

Q-"What if I want to, but just can't?"

A-Sometimes doing the right thing while your mind is DRAGGING, MAD, or hurting may require A LOT of persistence and SUFFERING; but the more often you work through it, the more often you will consistently feel good about yourself!

That's why we're starting small!

Your mind can literally be saying, "No, I just CAN'T" and you can still bend down and pick up or put away one thing. You're not expected to suddenly do everything right all the time; you're just beginning to begin a new habit! A small habit that can grow and then become a **NEW NORMAL**!

Even if you literally only do the right thing once a day for YEARS, you'll still be much better off than just continuing on autopilot. Once a day will make you feel better, and the better you feel about yourself, the more often you'll find yourself having INTEGRITY and doing what's right.

You can create an UPWARD SPIRAL instead of a downward spiral! You do good so you feel good, and because you feel good you do good, and because you do good you feel good, and etc....

You're ACTIONS teach you to feel like you deserve the success you seek, and you will also start to find you feel HAPPY for no specific reason.

Follow through on your INTEGRITY Habit AT LEAST once a day at work, school, or at home. SMILE and DO WHAT'S RIGHT NO MATTER HOW YOU FEEL; feel silly, dumb, mad, lazy, and DO IT ANYWAY AT LEAST ONCE A DAY! Do it ESPECIALLY WHEN YOU DON'T FEEL LIKE IT!

I'm not trying to be cruel; I'm just being **BRUTALLY KIND.**

That's why you're here, isn't it?

SERIOUSLY! ONCE A DAY IS ALL YOU NEED TO DO for now! If you skipped it earlier, go back and fill out the commitment form! If you haven't performed your first ACT OF INTEGRITY, do it now!

Regardless of whether or not you ever take my advice, you are still A GOOD PERSON to me!

You always will be!

"The weak can never forgive. Forgiveness is the attribute of the strong."

-Mahatma Gandhi

Chapter 10 FORGIVENESS

The previous chapters have a lot of common knowledge in them.

Even before you read them, if I was to format the following statements as true or false test questions, nearly everyone would get them all correct. In fact, let's try it!

For each statement, answer either true or false.

_____ Money and things can't buy happiness

_____ Goals for the future help us do better work in the present

_____ We should do what's right no matter how we feel

_____ Our emotions can get us in trouble if we let them control us

We didn't have to read the proceeding chapters to know that all the answers to these questions are true instead of false. For big decisions, public decisions where all eyes are on us, most of us would probably use those truths to guide us, **but why don't we live that way every day?**

The problem lies in our automatic negative beliefs (yes, more conditioning) we have about ourselves and others. We've mostly gone on AUTO PILOT, and acted bad and done bad things so long, that deep down many of us don't think very highly of ourselves.

I'm bringing this up now because unless you learn what is in this chapter, all the things that have come before about being GRATEFUL, being FUTURE FOCUSED, and having INTEGRITY will quickly fade! If deep down part of you believes you're a BAD person, it will be extremely difficult to ACT RIGHT long-term!

If you've ever done a weekend seminar or religious retreat, you know exactly what I'm talking about. When you leave those weekends of positivity and excitement, you usually feel uplifted, strong, and full of knowledge and wisdom that should affect you for the rest of your life. But most of the time, after just a few days or weeks, we go back to our old normal behavior. The emotional high has faded, and all those truths, good intentions, and commitments are mostly forgotten because once they're not NEW anymore, our minds discard them. They're like old helium balloons left over from a party, still barely floating above the floor.

So, how do you make new habits that stick? How do you change your automatic negative thinking?

The only answer I've found is FORGIVENESS. When you FORGIVE, it opens you heart and mind. FORGIVE yourself for your bad habits, bad thoughts, and bad decisions; and FORGIVE your family, friends, and enemies, too!

FORGIVE anything you're still upset about from the past ON PURPOSE as many times as needed, because FORGIVENESS is the MOST IMPORTANT KEY to HAPPINESS and to LONG-TERM CHANGE!

Yes, I said FORGIVENESS IS THE KEY TO CHANGE because it changes how we think!

When we FORGIVE, we become **CLEAR 2 LEARN! CLEAR2LEARN means you're thinking clearly rather than emotionally!** You're able to look for the best, honest way to respond or act, instead of letting your emotions or negativity tell you what to do.

So, here it is in a nutshell!

Key to Happiness 4:

FORGIVE the past so you can be HAPPY in the present!

When we're angry, or upset we can't think straight, so instead of trying to help make a situation better, we're trying to get even! Instead of trying to resolve the problem, we're DRAGGING or trying to get PAYBACK!

Despite what we've all been raised to believe, long-term change will NEVER happen as long as we're mad or upset!

Not all families, offices, or classrooms are warzones, but most do have some level of upset that seems normal and keeps everyone far less happy with their lives and relationships than they could be! Without ever meaning to, most of us at home, and at work or school have created and perpetuated vicious cycles of negativity.

I call that cycle THE PUNISHMENT AND PAYBACK LOOP!

You might get your way today, but there can be no lasting victory because as soon as someone "wins," the other person is looking to get payback, and usually neither of them is even aware of what they're really doing!

Back and forth, we take turns hurting each other, just like my father and me. One thinks, "You're lazy, so I'm going to be mean!" and then the other responds with, "You're mean so I'm going to be lazy!" Nobody can be happy for very long because for one person to win means the other person loses and then the loser feels justified in paying the other back!

The good news is that the PUNISHMENT and PAYBACK LOOP only continues as long as both sides are doing it!

FORGIVING yourself or others for being a mean and bossy jerk or a sneaky and lazy creep is like pushing a reset button!

You become CLEAR 2 LEARN and it allows you to see real people again and not just the personifications of all the negative beliefs you've built up in your mind. It means instead of paying someone back, you'll be willing to let it go, start fresh, and focus on maintaining your own INTEGRITY!

Only one person has to become CLEAR 2 LEARN for these changes to start! Remember, PUNISHMENT and PAYBACK is a partnership and it will only perpetuate if two people continue it. One person can break that cycle, **and since you're the one reading this book, that person is YOU!**

It's time for our MOST IMPORTANT HABIT FOR HAPPINESS, the one practice that can keep you CLEAR 2 LEARN, focused on INTEGRITY, positive in your relationships, and bring you success for <u>THE REST OF YOUR LIFE!</u>

So here's how it works: Who is that one person who hurts or aggravates you on a regular basis? It's probably someone close like a parent, teacher, boss, spouse, or child. Think about what that person does or has done and get ready to **FORGIVE!**

Keep in mind, you can feel hurt, or angry and still do it! You know how to SUFFER!

And yes, you can wait and do it later, but NOW is always the best time! Now is a good time to SUFFER, SMILE, and DO WHAT'S RIGHT no matter how you feel! If you're around people and feel embarrassed, go into the bathroom and close the door and flush right when you start to speak! *Or, of course, you don't have to say the words out loud!*

The Practice of <u>PURPOSEFUL FORGIVENESS</u>

1. **SMILE (yes, SUFFER and fake it if you have to!)**
2. **PUT *YOUR HAND ON YOUR HEART* and think about something this person has done, and how this person has acted…. Ready? GOOD!**
3. **SAY THE WORDS: "I forgive _____ for _____ and for being …. (Tell how that person was acting; it could be something like being a bully, a wimp, lazy or bossy, etc.…)**

74

4. (If you have faith in a higher power, you can also ask God to forgive that person, too!)
5. SAY THE WORDS (optional)
6. "I pray and ask God to forgive me/her/him, too."
7. Take a deep breath
8. Close your hand into a fist
9. Swing your fist out in front of you
10. Say, "as I hope (and pray) to be forgiven, so will I forgive."
11. Open your hand palm up to the sky and
12. Symbolically release whatever you've been holding onto
13. Take some more deep breaths.

You may feel a sense of release or a feeling of "unclenching" in your heart and soul! When this happens, you are becoming CLEAR 2 LEARN! I think it's your subconscious mind (and your amygdala; the part of your brain that controls, among other things, fearful and anxious emotions) reacting to your words and actions, and it's the first step towards seeing that person you've been upset with in a whole new light.

Did you forgive and notice a difference? Post about it on social media! #forgiveness #Brutal Kindness

If you continue with this practice of PURPOSEFUL FORGIVENESS over time, it can make a huge difference in your relationships and life! I promise you it has truly transformed mine!

FORGIVENESS

"HOW?" "WHY?"
Besides clearing the mental list of all your upsets,
FORGIVING also goes hand in hand with your first three
HABITS FOR HAPPINESS.

It's easier maintain an ATTITUDE of GRATITUDE, be
FUTURE FOCUSED, and have INTEGRITY when you're <u>NOT</u>
holding onto the hurts and grudges of the past! You can let
go of your conditioning more easily if you've FORGIVEN
yourself for all the bad or stupid things you've done.

Think about it; WHAT KIND OF PERSON...

-Is GRATEFUL and THANKFUL

-has good goals and is FUTURE FOCUSED

-DOES WHAT'S RIGHT NO MATTER HOW HE OR SHE FEELS!

- Lets go of anger and FORGIVES regularly ON PURPOSE?

Right, a GOOD PERSON and everybody knows GOOD
PEOPLE DESERVE TO BE HAPPY!

How do I know this? Because I've seen it happen again and
again with family, employees, friends, and students.
Because I'm living proof!

The person that most helped me learn to live this way was
my father.

"Darkness cannot drive out darkness; only light can do that. Hate cannot drive out hate; only love can do that."

-Martin Luther King, Jr.

Chapter 11 FORGIVENESS and Me

I could go on and on about why you should begin to FORGIVE on purpose. Here's my main reason: **I learned to be happy and successful, and love and get along with my ANGRY, bitter father.**

As a child, he was my mean, perfectionist, task master who was never satisfied with anything I did. He ruled by fear and I knew that if I stepped out of line, I was going to at least be yelled at and more than likely hit. As an adult, he offended, aggravated, and annoyed my first wife and me every time we were around him.

We argued and disagreed so much, and things got so bad that **we didn't speak to each other for over FIVE YEARS.**

Angry, overweight, and depressed, I saw therapists, psychologists, and psychiatrists. I was prescribed and took several different anti-depressant medicines, but none of them helped for very long.

Finally, I did a religious retreat through my church and they focused a lot on FORGIVENESS.

On the third day, with about 60 other men as witnesses, I burst into tears and cried on someone's shoulder because it suddenly hit me how much anger and sadness I had connected to my father.

I followed the advice of the leaders and began forgiving him and praying for him, asking God to guide us and bless us. FORGIVENESS and God's guidance helped me see that my mean, angry, bitter father was not the only jerk; I had done many mean and sneaky things to get back at him, but I had been too angry and hurt to see my own bad behavior!

After the retreat, I began to purposefully FORGIVE the past. Anytime I remembered something he did that made me mad or sad, or anything I'd done that I was ashamed of or felt bad about, I'd say the words, "I FORGIVE _____ for..." Then, I'd pray for guidance, and health and happiness.

It wasn't until I really began to focus on FORGIVENESS that I realized how many things I was upset about! Of course, there were all the hurts from Dad, but I also had anger towards my mother and myself because there were so many times we didn't or couldn't do anything about how he was treating us. There were also memories of mean teachers and bosses, ex-friends and ex-girlfriends, and there were plenty of stupid, sneaky, and bad things I'd done, too!

Some days, there were so many bad memories in my mind; it was as if they were all lined up for confession at church, just waiting for their turn to be FORGIVEN.

Other days I'd feel fine, but then I'd hear something or see something that reminded me of the past and I'd be angry again like it just happened; or I'd do something thoughtless or stupid in the present and then I'd be MAD at myself! I'd then take deep breaths and FORGIVE myself and those things, too!

Regardless of how many bad things I remembered, I SUFFERED and continued to FORGIVE them every day until there was basically nothing left. I DIDN'T REALIZE IT THEN, BUT I WAS BECOMING CLEAR 2 LEARN! FORGIVENESS and my belief in God and His guidance, were teaching me to see things differently!

It was just a few months later that I went and saw Dad for the first time in over five years. I apologized for the things I'd said and done, and he listened. He admitted that I wasn't the only one at fault and we left it at that.

I started going over and visiting my parents again, and even though he was still a picky, complaining, perfectionist, forgiveness made it easier to ACT RIGHT around him anyway. Because I had FORGIVEN him and myself, I was no longer trying to PAY HIM BACK for all the past hurts.

If I messed up (I still struggle with being on time!) and he called me out on it, I'd APOLOGIZE right away! At first, it FREAKED HIM OUT! He'd literally do a double-take when, instead of arguing or making excuses, I'd say "You're right! It was my fault! I should have paid closer attention! I'm sorry. I apologize!"

I swear he looked at me as if I'd just told him I was from another planet! Then he'd say, "No, no, don't worry about it! It's okay!" but I did worry, and I continued to apologize until he'd accept it!

The more I had INTEGRITY and showed him through my ACTIONS that I was a better person than he thought I was, the more he started to change how he saw me and treated me, too!

But here's the BRUTAL TRUTH: I had to be first!

I had to be the one to FORGIVE FIRST, APOLOGIZE FIRST, and HAVE INTEGRITY FIRST! When it comes to your parents or other authority figures in your life, the same will probably be true for you!

Your parents/older family members see themselves as the bosses and in the right because they are in positions of authority. They have made sacrifices for you, fed you, clothed you, and raised you, so they will probably not apologize first!

IT'S UP TO YOU TO SUFFER, ACT LIKE A GOOD PERSON, and start to break out of that vicious cycle of PUNISHMENT and PAYBACK.

Regardless of any mistakes they have made in the past, you'll be better off making the effort to FORGIVE NOW so you'll become CLEAR 2 LEARN and start ACTING and treating them differently. Eventually it will make a difference! It definitely did for me!

Anyway, back to me and Dad!

Since I had FORGIVEN him, I was no longer waiting and expecting him to act like a jerk so I could have another reason to get mad again! When he did say or do things that were rude or mean, I'd shrug them off because I was no longer feeling like a victim and I had nothing to prove and no reason to argue.

I started thinking, "Let the old man fuss and complain! Who cares! That's just the way he is." I just let him say what he wanted and mostly I didn't react or respond, other than to say, "Okay, Dad, I get it. I understand."

I'd be lying if I said this all happened overnight, one step right after another! There were times when we still lost our tempers with each other, especially towards the beginning, but usually I'd pray, FORGIVE, and then swallow my pride and go apologize again.

It took a few months before things really turned around. I tried my best to always be on time and do what I'd said I'd do, so his beliefs about me continued to change for the better! It got to where no matter what he was complaining about, if it was related to me, I'd APOLOGIZE and try to fix whatever it was.

Soon, he wasn't complaining about me much, but he was still a fussy old man! I used to HATE IT when he'd start complaining and fussing, going on and on about whatever caught his attention on the news, people he'd seen at a store, or something my mother or sister did, etc.... After I'd FORGIVEN him and the past, instead of getting frustrated and arguing or complaining back at him, I'd start to smile at him, chuckle, and then laugh!

81

Then the MAGIC HAPPENED.

Once I wasn't so hurt by and angry with him, it was actually kind of funny the way he went on and on about whatever annoyed him. (If you've ever seen the "Grumpy Old Men," movies, you know exactly what I'm talking about!)

Because I thought it was so funny, eventually so did he! He'd start chuckling and then laughing as he complained, too! He might still pretend to be mad at me for laughing, and raise his hand to smack me one, but he was smiling and doing it as a joke and I found that funny, too! The more I went out of my way to have INTEGRITY and be sincerely KIND to him, the more it affected him, too!

Soon, he was going out of his way to be sincerely KIND to me! He'd get me little gifts for no reason and started treating me differently. He'd say, "Steven, I saw this travel coffee cup in the markdown bin at the store and I know you drive a lot, so I got it for you!" He started calling me Mijo again. Mijo, pronounced "mee-ho," is a term of endearment that means "my son," in Spanish, and it was something he hadn't really called me since I was 9 or 10. He started saying things like, "Mijo, I told your mother you're coming over, so she's making your favorite enchiladas (cheese and onion!) for lunch."

As he got older, he relied on me more and more. He was always asking me for help. "Steven, can you help me fix the door? It's dragging again." Or "Mijo, come help me put in this new space heater; I can't get the connections right."

Already in his late 70's and me in my mid 30's, my once angry and critical father would watch me work, sitting in silence like he was watching a ball game, because he KNEW I was a person of INTEGRITY and I would get things done. Afterwards, he'd thank me for helping him and hug me.

In case it isn't obvious, that was NOT the way things worked for us in the past! That interaction NEVER could have happened that way if I hadn't learned how to have INTEGRITY, APOLOGIZE and FORGIVE!

This continued for the rest of his life. He turned 83 years old just a few weeks before he died.

The Beginning of the End

In his 80's he was no longer driving, so he'd walk or take the bus when my sister or I wasn't around to give him rides. He was on a busy 7 lane street (it had 3 lanes going each way and a turn lane in the middle) when he decided to cross. He stepped off the sidewalk and into the oncoming traffic. Tires squealed and screeched, but he made it past the first two lanes.

Then it happened! **"WHAM!"**

He got hit by a Ford F-250 going over fifty miles an hour. He was thrown all the way across the street and landed in a bloody heap on the opposite sidewalk. Even though he had suffered a massive trauma and had over 30 broken bones, that tough old man never lost consciousness and told people at the scene he just wanted to go home.

He lived three days after that. My mother, my sister, and I were able to sit with him, talk to him, and hold his hand until he was gone.

I can only imagine how differently I would have felt if I had still been holding onto all that anger and guilt. I can only imagine how his death would still haunt me.

I know that the anger and sadness that was tied to all those memories would only have gotten worse! There would have been yet another layer of guilt as well as a layer of regret heaped upon everything else, because it was too late to make changes and that broken relationship could now never be mended.

But that didn't happen! All the past was already FORGIVEN! Yes, I was surprised, hurt, and saddened by the tragic accident that ended his life, but I knew he led a good life overall! In his 83 years, he lived, worked, loved, married, raised children and got to know his grandchildren. What more can any of us ask for?

By FORGIVING him I came to realize that negative emotions aren't wrong and I'm not bad for having them! They're just part of life and I can use them to hurt or to help, to do bad or do good; the choice is always mine!

Now I mostly smile when I think of the things he'd say or how he'd act. I tell stories of our epic battles to make me work, and I make my friends and students laugh hysterically.

Forgiveness made all that possible! And trust me, during the process, I didn't always FEEL LIKE IT! There were many times I had to SUFFER and DO WHAT'S RIGHT NO MATTER HOW I FELT! Sometimes I FORGAVE with tears running down my face, or my teeth grit and my fists clenched, but I SUFFERED and did it anyway!

Some memories had to be FORGIVEN more than once because they made such an impression on me! I said the words, "I FORGIVE my father for hitting me, for laughing at me, for yelling at me! For being a cruel bully and a mean jerk," over and over again.

I still live this way! I can be reading a book, or driving to work, and if I suddenly remember something that I'm still hurting over, I immediately forgive that, too.

And so can you!

PURPOSEFUL FORGIVENESS

So, especially if you haven't done it yet, it's time to start forgiving the people you're mad at and start clearing up that backlog of old hurts!

It's time to learn to put your lifetime of conditioning aside and become CLEAR 2 LEARN! Yes, you may have to SUFFER and be **BRUTALLY KIND** to yourself to do it, but once you do, you'll start to see your husband, wife, child, parent, employee, student, or partner as a GOOD PERSON instead of a lazy idiot, sneaky creep, or mean enemy. You'll remember the things you love about them instead of just watching and waiting for them to make their next mistake.

Keep in mind, FORGIVENESS doesn't mean you have to welcome people who are extremely negative and hurtful back into your life! Some people are such a mess or so toxic, you really are better off without them!

Once you are CLEAR 2 LEARN, you will decide that for yourself on a case by case basis. YOU'RE A GOOD PERSON and FORGIVENESS will help you see the path that's best for you.

Most importantly, FORGIVING and becoming CLEAR 2 LEARN will give you the mental balance you need to think and react thoughtfully with ALL the people you encounter in your life today and in the future. You'll be kinder and stronger, and look for the good in people instead of the bad.

Your FORGIVENESS ALSO CREATES POSITIVE EXPECTATIONS, and your expectations make more of a difference than you can possibly know until you've experienced it for yourself! When I smile and treat people like GOOD PEOPLE, they usually go out of their way to make me right! Sadly, the same also happens when you think people are bad, too!

Having said that, it's time practice FORGIVENESS! Who or what have you not forgiven? Got something in mind? Good! Turn the page to begin!

The Practice of PURPOSEFUL FORGIVENESS

1. SMILE (yes, SUFFER and fake it if you have to!)
2. PUT *YOUR HAND ON YOUR HEART* and think about something this person has done, and how this person has acted.... Ready? GOOD!
3. SAY THE WORDS: "I forgive _____ for _____ and for being .... (Tell how that person was acting; it could be something like being a bully, a wimp, lazy or bossy, etc....)
4. Repeat the Above FORGIVENESS statement as many times as you need to with any other issues or people you're upset about/with!
5. (If you have faith in a higher power, you can also ask God to forgive that person, too!)
6. SAY THE WORDS (optional)
7. "I pray and ask God to forgive me/her/him, too."
8. Take a deep breath
9. Close your hand into a fist
10. Swing your fist out in front of you
11. Say, "as I hope (and pray) to be forgiven, so will I forgive."
12. Open your hand palm up to the sky and
13. Symbolically release whatever you've been holding onto
14. Take some more deep breaths.

EXCELLENT! Do you feel better? Lighter? You're on the path to becoming CLEAR 2 LEARN! Keep FORGIVING until you feel CLEAR!

This is just the start!

It's time to commit to our MOST IMPORTANT HABIT FOR HAPPINESS!

Habit for Happiness 4:

PURPOSEFUL FORGIVENESS

I, _____, commit to FORGIVE! Whenever I feel sad, mad, scared, or bad, I'm going to say the words and FORGIVE who and what I'm upset about. I'll FORGIVE so my ACTIONS will teach me to see myself as a GOOD PERSON and others as GOOD PEOPLE.

Signed: _____ Dated: _____

Did you fill it out? **EXCELLENT!** Post about it on social media! #forgiveness #Brutal Kindness

Remember, <u>ANY TIME</u> you're mad, sad, afraid, or feel bad, you'll ask yourself, "What needs to be FORGIVEN?" And then follow the steps on the previous page!

If you're anything like me, at first you'll find that you'll need to FORGIVE many times a day. After several months of PURPOSEFUL FORGIVENESS, my thinking changed! I no longer needed psychological help or depression medication, and I began putting my life together again.

Are you holding back? Do you feel like you just can't or won't do what I've asked you to do? I understand. Look over the statements and responses and read whatever will benefit you the most.

-"But you don't understand; I CAN'T FORGIVE!"
For the majority of us, YES YOU CAN! More than likely, you're DRAGGING right now! You're so used to being angry and hurt that it feels WRONG to let it go! You've probably been angry and hurt so long it's normal to have that part of your heart and mind closed off, but you won't be able to sustain a life of HAPPINESS and INTEGRITY if you don't FORGIVE!

If you have one thing in particular that you can't deal with, then you can always skip over that for now! Focus on smaller things, on the people who are annoying and bothersome instead of that person who broke your heart! Come back to that big thing later!

Go back to **PURPOSEFUL FORGIVENESS** and go through the steps! You'll be glad you did!

If you flat out just feel like you CAN'T FORGIVE, then don't listen to me, and please see a mental healthcare professional! If you are already under the care of a mental health professional, then follow his or her advice! Come back to this if or when you feel well enough and have the approval of your mental healthcare provider.

-"Yeah, but seriously, I have to feel it and I just don't!"
Remember, FEELINGS ARE NOT THE TRUTH! Your feelings are tied to rebellion and DRAGGING, or being angry and MAD! They don't have to be in control! You can still say the words no matter how you feel.

If you say the words often enough your feelings will catch up! If you don't say the words, you might NEVER feel like it; especially if you've been holding onto this anger or hurt for a long time. If you have to SMILE, and SUFFER to do it, then do that! You'll be glad you did!

If I had learned to do PURPOSEFUL FORGIVENESS in high school, my life would have been so much better! I would have DRAGGED much less, gotten in less trouble, and been more successful. I'd of had more fun and peace with Dad and more success at work!

You can't change your past any more than I can, but you can make choices NOW that will affect your present and future!

You may have to SUFFER to do it, but you know how to do that! You're a GOOD PERSON and know how to ACT WITH INTEGRITY! I say, go back a few pages to PURPOSEFUL FORGIVENESS and say the words EVEN IF YOU DON'T FEEL THEM! Saying the words, especially when you don't feel them, will teach your mind to start thinking and seeing things differently!

-"That person is STILL hurting me!"
If you're in an abusive relationship or have an abusive family member, then YES, do what you can to get help and

get out as soon as you can! (You can call the National Domestic Violence Hotline at 1-800-799-7233!) Care enough about you to reach out for help and keep asking even if it makes people uncomfortable!

If you're like me and have someone in your life that is a bully or mean, but not to the point that it could be proven as abuse, you may just have to keep moving forward with your life as you best you can, and FORGIVENESS, along with the other Habits for Happiness, can help you do that! NO, IT'S NOT YOUR FAULT that your family treats you bad; but you may have no idea how much you are contributing to a negative family dynamic until you can look at things without your emotions controlling you! FORGIVING and becoming CLEAR 2 LEARN can help you just like it did me with my father!

Dropping out of school or quitting a job? Moving out, divorcing, or kicking someone out? Why not make one last-ditch effort to begin a habit of FORGIVENESS, and consider the possibility that as long as we hold onto anger and upset our emotions are controlling us and we're not thinking straight.

Go back to **PURPOSEFUL FORGIVENESS** and go through the steps! You'll be glad you did!

-"But I've already messed up too much!"

Many of us are much harder on ourselves than on anyone else! We have done things that we consider to be shameful and unforgiveable and we just don't know how to let them go! Feeling BAD about yourself can become just as much a habit as being MAD or DRAGGING! You may have to just SUFFER and do it on purpose!

Here's the BRUTAL TRUTH: Living with a belief that you're BAD and don't deserve FORGIVENESS will only make things WORSE! Even if you really don't deserve FORGIVENESS, the people who know and love you deserve better! I treat my wife, my kids, and my students better because I've FORGIVEN and feel better about myself. They deserve the best of me, even if I don't!

It's the same for you! Are you going to punish everyone in your life because you messed up in the past? You can if you really want to, but what good would that do? When it comes to FORGIVENESS, just like with anything else, the choice is always up to you! If you're thinking I might be on to something, but you're hesitant to try, I say it's time to take a leap of faith! Do it for you and the people you love!

Remember, YOUR FEELINGS, THOUGHT, AND EMOTIONS ARE NOT THE TRUTH! DESPITE YOUR CONDITIONING, YOU CAN DO GOOD WHILE YOU STILL FEEL BAD! SUFFER TO DO WHAT'S RIGHT!

Now is the time to build your INTEGRITY muscle! Smile, SUFFER, go back to PURPOSEFUL FORGIVENESS and go through the steps! You'll be glad you did!

"In order to carry a positive action we must develop here a positive vision."

-the Dalai Lama

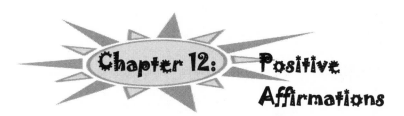

Chapter 12: Positive Affirmations

Have you noticed that you don't try things because you're not confident you can be good at them? Have there been times when you struggle, and then quit or fail? Maybe you've never really thought about it before, but I want you to think about it now. What goes through your mind when you're upset with yourself or others, or when you try something new?

Think about the last time you REALLY messed up and the things you automatically say to yourself in your head: maybe you found yourself thinking things like...

1. **"My boss/teacher/parent/child hates me!"**
2. **"I'm such a mess!"**
3. **"I hate school/my job!"**
4. **"I'm so stupid!"**
5. **"I can't believe I messed up AGAIN!"**
6. **"Why does this ALWAYS happen to me!"**

If you think about it and realize that you do have negative thoughts and self-talk, then also realize that those negative thoughts are part of what has caused you to fail.

Like with most of the other negative things we do, we usually aren't even aware of what we're doing! We don't even realize we're on AUTOPILOT and talking ourselves into being disappointed and upset, but every time we automatically say or think things like "I can't do it!" "I'm such a screw up!" or "This is too hard! I QUIT!" we are reinforcing a mindset of failure and the negative beliefs we ALREADY have about ourselves.

If you find yourself struggling with achieving your goals or being positive on purpose, POSITIVE AFFIRMATIONS can really help; ESPECIALLY if you're already practicing GRATTITUDE, INTEGRITY, and FORGIVENESS!

From the age of 5 or 6 up to my mid 30's, I really was a lazy, selfish, sneaky, weak, no good liar! The main problem was, like I've said before, that I didn't realize it then! I just thought I had bad luck and when I did bad or stupid things, I blamed them on my parents and my "horrible childhood."

I would be lazy and distracted, then realize I was running late and get MAD at myself! I'd leave in a huge rush, speeding and running stop lights to try to make up time! I got where I was going late about half the time, and when I was late I'd usually lie or exaggerate about how bad traffic was to cover for myself.

Once I got started working, I usually worked pretty slow until the deadline got close or someone fussed at me! Then, you guessed it, I'd get MAD at myself and push myself to catch up! I was, and still am, a quick thinker and very creative, so sometimes I really did beautiful work, but

I did it in spite of my negative automatic habits, and I wasn't consistent.

Do you recognize a pattern? Me, too! I was programmed to be lazy, so I DRAGGED; and then when I realized I was messing up, I got MAD at myself and pushed myself to catch up. This happened over and over again because I had fallen into a PUNISHMENT AND PAYBACK LOOP WITH MYSELF! I managed to meet my deadlines about 70-80% of the time, but I was ALWAYS stressed out and on the verge of screwing up!

Living that way usually worked well enough to keep me from getting fired, but it also kept me feeling bad about myself; it also meant my bosses were sometimes disappointed, and they were losing respect for me, too.

I'm sure I'm not the only person who's ever been at war with himself or herself! If you recognize yourself in my example, GOOD! That's the first step towards being able to do something about it!

Once you've FORGIVEN yourself for being the way you've been conditioned to be, and you've become CLEAR2LEARN; creating POSITIVE AFFIRMATIONS allows you to LITERALLY change your thinking! Instead of repeating your old normal negative thoughts and words you've been conditioned to say, you will create new things to say to yourself that will help you move in the right direction and retrain yourself to be more successful!

Here are some of my POSITIVE AFFIRMATIONS:
1. **"I love writing!"**
2. **"Writing makes me happy!"**

3. "I love being on time!"
4. "I am a best-selling author!"
5. "I love being successful"
6. "I'm happy, healthy, successful, and strong!"

So, now it's time to think about what you're struggling with. Here are some examples:

1. running late
2. missing deadlines
3. Forgetting or losing things
4. Calling in sick/being absent
5. falling behind/procrastinating
6. getting too emotional (angry, sad, nervous, etc....)
7. conflicts with others (bosses, teachers, coworkers, etc....)

What are the main issues that might make success more difficult for you?

If you're thinking, "What issues? Things are just fine!" then remember that you don't have to act perfect! Nobody is trying to put you down or make you feel bad!

Anyway, now to do some writing! Turn the page and write about what are you struggling with, and what is slowing you down, or getting in the way of your success. As usual, spelling and grammar don't matter! Just write about what's on your mind!

Reflection 4: Where can Positive Affirmations Help me?

What bad habit(s)do you have? What might get in the way of accomplishing your goals? Explain.

How do you feel when you're struggling?

What do you think to yourself when you're struggling? Explain.

You're done? GREAT WORK! Writing about your struggles has probably stirred up your memories and emotions! It's time to practice PURPOSEFUL FORGIVENESS so you can become CLEAR 2 LEARN! Think about the times you've messed up, and the things you've done that have kept you from becoming as successful as you could be!

Ready? Good! Turn the page!

The Practice of PURPOSEFUL FORGIVENESS

1. SMILE (yes, SUFFER and fake it if you have to!)
2. PUT *YOUR HAND ON YOUR HEART* and think about something you have done, and how you've acted…. Ready? GOOD!
3. SAY THE WORDS: "I forgive _____ for _____and for being …. (Tell how you were acting; it could be something like being a bully, a wimp, lazy or bossy, etc.…)
4. Repeat the Above FORGIVENESS statement as many times as you need to with any other issues or people you're upset about or with!
5. If you have faith in a higher power, you can also ask God to forgive that person, too!
6. SAY THE WORDS (optional)
7. "I pray and ask God to forgive me/her/him, too."
8. Take a deep breath
9. Close your hand into a fist
10. Swing your fist out in front of you
11. Say, "as I hope (and pray) to be forgiven, so will I forgive."
12. Open your hand palm up to the sky and
13. Symbolically release whatever you've been holding onto
14. Take some more deep breaths.

If you left someone or something off, go through the process again until you feel CLEAR.

Now, let's come up with some affirmations for you! The key is talking about what you want as if it's what you already have or are. For me, being on time has ALWAYS been an issue. Instead of saying, "I don't want to be late anymore," I say, **"I LOVE BEING ON TIME! I am punctual, successful, and organized. I LOVE BEING ON TIME! IT MAKES ME HAPPY!"**

You may feel awkward at first, **but SUFFER and say them anyway!** Positive words, said aloud and silently over and over again, nudged me to change my behaviors without me even having to think about what I'm doing differently! Instead of struggling and fighting with myself to be on time, my ACTIONS changed to match my words and thoughts so that now days I'm regularly on time! Try it for yourself! Let's create some affirmations that will help you!

My POSITIVE AFFIRMATIONS

-To replace automatic negative talk/ behaviors with positive ones, fill in the blank with your Career: (entrepreneur, lawyer, teacher, attorney....etc)

"I am a successful, smart, _____!

Being a _____ makes me HAPPY"

- Fill in the blanks to create New GOOD Habits (on time, organized, happy, etc....)

"I LOVE being _____!
It makes me HAPPY" (say again as needed for all wanted behaviors!)

Done? EXCELLENT! YOU ROCK! Post your affirmations on social media with #PositiveAffirmations!

Positive Affirmations in ACTION

I've had students who've HATED a class (usually it was biology, geography, or chemistry), so I coached them to say, "I LOVE CHEMISTRY! It's FUN and I'm SMART!" Or students who were terrible test takers and usually failed them, so I coached them to say "I LOVE TESTING! I'm SMART AND SUCCESFUL!"

Many times, they'd want to argue about it or not do what I asked! Some would say, "NO! SERIOSLY! I HATE THAT CLASS!" To which I'd reply, "I know! That's part of the problem!" If I had to, I'd give them "the look" like I was going to burn a hole through their head with my eyes, (one student calls it, "the death stare") and I'd say, "GOOD! SUFFER and DO IT ANYWAY!"

The first time saying it was the hardest and then it got easier with practice. Soon after, many of them passed tests for the first time in the classes they were struggling with!

One student actually ran to my room yelling, "Mr. Carvajal! I made an 87! An 87! I've NEVER EVEN PASSED A TEST in that class before!"

I even had a student who was trying out to be a cheerleader. She was so nervous and worried she literally couldn't sit still and do her work because she was so afraid she was going to mess up her audition! I coached her to say, "I LOVE BEING SUCCESSFUL! I'M CONFIDENT, CALM, and STRONG!" She rolled her eyes at me and fussed that she didn't have time and couldn't think about that right now, but eventually she did it anyway. The next day I found out her audition went very well! She became a cheerleader and recently won an award for being cheerleader of the week!

My POSITIVE AFFIRMATIONS really made a difference for me! When I combined them with all the other HABITS FOR HAPPINESS, they changed my life, my relationships, and my level of success for the better!

These days I'm pretty much talking to myself all the time. In my head, I'm saying my AFFIRMATIONS as I get ready for school. Instead of zoning out and then realizing I'm running late AGAIN, I'm focused and guided by my words. Instead of worrying about all the things I need to do that morning and should have done last night, I've already done them! I've already graded, planned, and prepped all the things I need for the day, so I'm ready for whatever new duty or challenge that arises.

When I mess up—**Yes, when not if! I'm NOT perfect!**— I SUFFER, APOLOGIZE, FORGIVE myself, and get right back on track! If I'm late, it's not by much, and I own up to it and apologize to whoever is in charge. Because I'm so honest and it's not often enough for anyone to feel like they have to straighten me out, I have a really good rapport with my bosses! My life works and my HABITS FOR HAPPINESS and my POSITIVE AFFIRMATIONS continue throughout the day, every day!

I'm saying POSITIVE AFFIRMATIONS as I exercise. "I love EXERCISING! I'm young, strong, happy, and healthy!"

I'm saying POSITIVE AFFIRMATIONS as I'm cleaning and organizing. "I LOVE BEING NEAT, CLEAN, and ORGANIZED! It makes me HAPPY!

I'm saying POSITIVE AFFIRMATIONS about teaching, writing, or anything else I'm doing that day like grading, filing, or planning.

Okay, so it's time to make this a regular part of your day! It's time to create your **FINAL HABIT FOR HAPPINESS!**

Purposeful Positivity Habit for Happiness 5:

Positive Affirmations

I, _____, commit to saying my POSITIVE AFFIRMATIONS AT LEAST once a day so I can reset my AUTOPILOT and move towards success! I can say them more often, especially when I'm struggling, but I will say them AT LEAST once a day no matter what!

Signed: _____ Dated: _____

Got it done? **EXCELLENT! You ROCK!**
Take a picture and upload it on social media with #PositiveAffirmations! If you haven't done it already, set an alarm on your phone so you will act on /do ALL your

HABITS FOR HAPPINESS, including saying your POSITIVE AFFIRMATIONS to yourself at least once a day.

Besides the ones you wrote, you can also use the AFFIRMATIONS on the next page. Keep creating more of your own as you need them. With your NEW NORMAL soundtrack of POSITIVE AFFIRMATIONS in your head to guide you and support you, you will move faster towards the FUTURE you created FOR YOURSELF in your "Me, 10 Years From Now" writing.

Turn the page and pick some you can use or adapt to your needs and wants!

SMILE and read!

For general success:

- "I am smart, successful, and confident."
- "I am strong, healthy, and calm."
- "I love being successful! It makes me HAPPY!"
- "I love accomplishing things! It makes me HAPPY!"
- "I love getting my work done! It makes me HAPPY!"

For replacing old bad habits:

- I'M A GOOD PERSON! I LOVE BEING ON TIME!
- I LOVE GETTING MY WORK DONE!
- I LOVE EATING HEALTHY FOOD!
- I'M A GOOD PERSON! I LOVE EXERCISING!
- I LOVE MYSELF! I'M A GOOD PERSON!
- I AM STRONG AND I GET THINGS DONE!

For creating positive interactions and teamwork:

- I LOVE MY FAMILY! They're GOOD PEOPLE!
- I LOVE MY _____ (wife, husband, son, mom, etc....) HE OR SHE IS A GOOD PERSON!
- I LOVE MY COWORKERS! We are a HAPPY, CONFIDENT, SUCCESSFUL TEAM!
- I'M A GOOD PERSON! I TREAT PEOPLE WITH RESPECT AND KINDNESS.
- I'M A GOOD PERSON! I EXPECT PEOPLE TO BE SUCCESSFUL!

Post your positive affirmations, or how POSITIVE AFFIRMATIONS have helped you with #PositiveAffirmations

"I do not think that there is any other quality so essential to success of any kind as the quality of perseverance. It overcomes almost everything, even nature."

-John D. Rockefeller

Chapter 13 Positivity FOR LIFE!

WE'RE ALMOST DONE! That's about all I have to offer in this book. The rest is about learning to keep going, refocusing, and getting back on track.

In our society, many of us believe that messing up or failing a time or two means that we either can't or won't be successful, so we should just quit. It's okay to feel bad and want to quit, BUT KEEP GOING ANYWAY! Remember, you can't control your feelings, but you can control your ACTIONS!

Keeping up with your HABITS FOR HAPPINESS is the best way to keep yourself on the right track. What makes them so easy to do is that they're quick and small! You don't need hours; you can do them ALL right after you wake up and set the tone for how you ACT throughout your day!

ACT like a GOOD PERSON! Once a day (or more if you feel like it)...

1. **Thank, compliment, or help someone**
2. **Be FUTURE FOCUSED and think about your goals**

3. SUFFER and do what's right no matter how you feel
4. Say your AFFIRMATIONS

If you stop and think about it, **THIS IS SO EASY!** You can do them all in under a minute! For example:

1. SMILE (yes, fake it if you have to!) and find someone to say or text, "Thanks for _____! I really appreciate it!"
2. "I'm going to do my best today so I can become a veterinarian!"
3. Wipe up that spill on the counter or put away those socks!
4. SMILE and say, "I am healthy, happy, and strong!" "I love being a kind and successful veterinarian!" (or whatever your FUTURE FOCUSED goal is!)

In each situation, you might often find yourself doing more, BUT YOU DON'T HAVE TO! On a bad day, or an extremely busy day, you may have to SUFFER to just do the minimum, but PURPOSEFULLY doing just the minimum will still keep POSITIVITY alive and growing in your mind!

Speaking of bad days, remember to **FORGIVE!** Whenever you feel sad, mad, afraid, or bad...

1. FORGIVE who (including you!) and/or what you're upset about! Remember, hand on heart, I Forgive.... (see pg. 85 for full wording) This will help you become CLEAR 2 LEARN.
2. REFLECT on and PROBLEM SOLVE for any issue or situation that keeps happening or coming up again and again.

Easy, right? Sure, but old habits don't just go away! We all know you can't erase a lifetime of conditioning (remember Pavlov's Dog?) by reading a book!

 And to that I say, **"SO WHAT!"**

Most of us are not steady, stay the course, people. We mess up, get distracted, bored, emotional, busy, etc…, and we lose track of what we planned and what we want. Before we know it, we're back to old habits, but we don't have to stay that way if we're willing to learn what I'm here to teach you. Learning this will make POSITIVITY yours <u>FOR LIFE!</u>

BRUTAL KINDNESS:

First, accept the fact that **YOU WILL MESS UP!**

Of course we don't like to think that way! We think, "No! I'm in this for LIFE! I know what to do and how to do it!"

Well, yes, and so do I, but I still have to SMILE, SUFFER and get myself back on track AT LEAST ONCE A WEEK! You'll probably have to do the same!

We all have those days when we're distracted! If you're anything like me, you probably won't even realize you messed up until it's almost too late.

You'll be ready to do your exercise or homework, or go to bed early so you can get up early and get things done, but something will happen: a friend texts and wants to hang out, your favorite show just came out with new episodes, or even something like your sister's car broke down and you need to help her.

Maybe you'll even tell yourself you're just going to play one game, or only watch one video, but before you know it, it's after midnight and you haven't done anything you said you were going to do!

What do you think usually happens, then?

Most people get mad at themselves, try again, fail again, and then give up because they think it's hopeless or too hard. But think about it: what happens when you push yourself and get mad at yourself?

Right! You got it! We get MAD because we're DRAGGING, and then we're DRAGGING because we're MAD. You will probably end up in a PUNISHMENT AND PAYBACK LOOP with yourself, and at best be sporadic in keeping up with your Habits, or at worst give up entirely.

How do you avoid that? No matter what, as soon as you realize what you're doing, FORGIVE, LEARN, and GET BACK TO WORK!

After all these years, I still want to do stupid, lazy, sneaky stuff, but most of the time I DO WHAT'S RIGHT anyway because I've learned how to keep going even if my emotions are out of control! I still get sad, afraid, or angry; and my mind will still tell me, "I just CAN'T!" but most of the time I SMILE, SUFFER, AND DO WHAT'S RIGHT NO MATTER HOW I FEEL!

Yes, every now and then I still miss a deadline, I do arrive late, I act mean and argue with my wife; but instead of seeing that as a reason to quit, **I FORGIVE, LEARN, and GET BACK ON TRACK!**

You can learn to do it, too! Whether it's the first time or the hundredth time, the answer is still the same: FORGIVE, LEARN, and GET BACK ON TRACK!

Maybe you're thinking, *"That's too easy!"*

Well, it's not!

Without even realizing it, your mind, trained by a lifetime of conditioning, will use your emotions to push you back to your old habits! It's like your subconscious mind believes that your old bad habits are reality and when you're following those old patterns, you're not doing anything! They're normal and the way things should be, so your mind will fight (DRAG or GET MAD) and try to make you go back to what it's used to. Your mind will use your emotions, trip you up and make you make dumb mistakes, and try to wear you down because it's used to feeling and thinking the way you've thought and felt for most of your life. **It's NOT because deep down you're bad, a loser, or dumb; it's because you're human and these responses are automatic!**

Even if you have to do it ten times a day every day for as long as you're still alive, you can still FORGIVE, LEARN, and GET BACK ON TRACK one more time! You can feel angry, sad, afraid, depressed, etc... and you can SUFFER and start doing the right thing over and over again as many times as you need to!

Your mind can think, "I QUIT!" and you can still...

1. <u>**FORGIVE ON PURPOSE:**</u> **Think about who or what you're upset about and what happened, and then**

practice PURPOSEFUL FORGIVENESS until you feel
CLEAR 2 LEARN

2. <u>LEARN</u>: REFLECT over what happened, why you're
so upset, and then problem solve so you won't get
stuck again.

3. <u>GET BACK ON TRACK</u>: Do your Daily HABITS FOR
HAPPINESS and then get back to work! Honoring
those small commitments will help you get
refocused faster than anything else!

You can do all of those things in just a couple of minutes,
so even if it is 2 AM, you can SUFFER and spend just a little
more time to get yourself on the road to feeling better and
happier!

If your emotions are REALLY STIRRED UP, it might feel like
TORTURE to fulfill your HABITS FOR HAPPINESS, but that's
just your subconscious mind clinging to your old normal
habits! **You know how to SUFFER!**

BRUTAL KINDNESS Q&A:

*Q -"But, what if I don't? What if instead of doing my habits,
I just go to sleep?"*

**A -Great, then in the morning it's time to FORGIVE, LEARN,
and GET BACK ON TRACK!**

*Q -"Yeah, but, what if I give up and just don't care and a
whole month passes and I'm basically living like I did before
I got started with all of this?"*

A -Great! Whenever you realize what you're doing and get tired of being miserable and having no INTEGRITY, it will be time to FORGIVE, LEARN, and GET BACK ON TRACK!

Q -"What if I really am just no good? What if I just can't do this?"

A -Then you really do believe that you're too lazy, too bad, and too undeserving of a good life! You're too upset with yourself and don't know how to get past it!

Go back to the FORGIVENESS chapter and work through it for your family and for everybody who cares about you! Even if you really do believe you don't deserve to have a happy life, don't punish everybody who loves you because you're no good! Start ACTING GOOD, and have faith that this process and your ACTIONS will teach you a better way to live and think over time.

Then, you guessed it; it's time to FORGIVE, LEARN, and GET BACK ON TRACK!

… Or give up and go back to your old way of life! You have to be the one to choose! I can't do it for you! If you do give up, remember that this book will still be here whenever you're ready to FORGIVE, LEARN, and GET BACK TO WORK!

The answer will always be the same whether it's been three days, three months, or even three years! EVERY DAY IS A NEW CHANCE TO START OVER! To SUFFER, SMILE, and do your daily HABITS FOR HAPPINESS, and then get back to ACTING RIGHT and living a happy and successful life!

Each time you do, you're retraining your brain to follow your NEW NORMAL! Remember, FORGIVENESS is the key to long term change! By forgiving yourself you are disrupting any PUNISHMENT and PAYBACK loop you may have fallen into! Instead of PUSHING and PUNISHING yourself you're MAD, you'll be redirecting and helping yourself because you CARE, so there's no need to rebel and DRAG or GET MAD and quit!

I'm SO PROUD OF YOU FOR READING THIS FAR! I'M SO PROUD OF YOU FOR BEING COACHABLE AND LEARNING WHAT I HAVE TO TEACH!

IMAGINE HOW MANY PEOPLE YOU CAN HELP IF THEY NOTICE A DIFFERENCE IN YOU?

You can always go to my website and find more tools for PURPOSEFUL POSITIVITY. Watch videos about the concepts you've learned and how to overcome automatic negativity! Tell us about your successes and your struggles on social media! #BrutalKindness, #integrity, or #suffer.

A wise friend once told me, "when you're feeling good, we need you; and when you're feeling bad, you need us!" Either way, keep coming back! I'll always be here for you!

Steve

"The first question which the priest and the Levite asked was: 'If I stop to help this man, what will happen to me?' But... the Good Samaritan reversed the question: 'If I do not stop to help this man, what will happen to him?'"   -Martin Luther King, Jr.

Thank you!

for reading and going through this process!

The above quote, by Dr. King, exemplifies the way of thinking that kept bringing me back and working on this regardless of how I felt!

As you practice living in INTEGRITY and all the other **HABITS FOR HAPPINESS,** your self-image will change for the better! Instead of being something to hide and be ashamed of, each new negative thing you recognize about yourself will become a new thing to **FORGIVE** and learn from. It will help you grow and bring you a deeper understanding of human nature, a greater sense of happiness, and a stronger sense of satisfaction with your family and friends, work and life. Your actions guided by INTEGRITY, and your attitude of purposeful positivity will also teach others to see themselves as better people, too!

KEEP IN MIND! You won't ALWAYS feel happy and successful! NOBODY DOES! That's when you refocus on your **HABITS FOR HAPPINESS** and **ACT RIGHT** no matter how you feel!

Remember to STAY HUMBLE! Once you've been doing this for a while, it can be very easy to feel superior to people who don't know what we know! We are not learning to live a life of **POSITIVITY** so we can look down on others! We are learning so we can help each other realize how good we ALL really are, and how happy we can ALL truly be.

If you notice that you're becoming prideful and condescending, FORGIVE YOURSELF and then SMILE, SUFFER, AND ACT RIGHT! I have to do just that pretty often!

Has learning to live a life of **POSITIVITY** helped you? Does it make you feel good to help others succeed? Yes, me too!

You must know by now that I'm lazy by nature! Thirty years of being pushed around by Dad means I'd much rather sit on the couch and watch TV or read, instead of trying to help more people in my free time!

Every year, I'd see kids struggling and think, I KNOW they would do be doing better if I was their teacher; but then, I'd tell myself, "There's only one of me! I can only do so much!"

But what if there wasn't only one of me?

What if these ways of thinking and acting could be spread by many?

Think about it:

- What WILL happen to all the "troubled kids" if things continued just the way they are?
- What COULD happen to all the "troubled kids" if EVERYBODY learned what we know?

The most important thing about living this kind of positive lifestyle is that with practice you can take this to the NEXT LEVEL and become **A FORCE OF POSITIVITY!**

Leading a **BRUTALLY KIND** life of **PURPOSEFUL POSITIVITY** will cause you to become a light in a dark world! The people around you will feel better and act better because of how you see them and treat them. They'll also see themselves as better people because you expect them to **ACT** like they deserve it!

If you have a great experience of being successful, or helping others, tell about it and help spread the word! Share it on social media! Tell us what happened and how things are different now! Your written or video testimony can be a huge help to those who are still negative and struggling! Here are some good hashtags to use:

#BrutalKindness   #suffer   #Integrity

#FutureFocused   #forgiveness   #Positivity

#PositiveOnPurpose   #Habits4Happiness

Speaking of being #FUTURE FOCUSED...

What would happen to our world if this way of thinking and acting actually became NORMAL! I don't just mean people who talk about change and love to repost quotes on wisdom and love on social media , but rather the majority of us ACTUALLY LIVING THEIR LIVES WITH INTEGRITY and FORGIVENESS as their guides and being CLEAR2LEARN as their normal state of being? Yes, you keep your beliefs and I keep mine, you be you and I'll be me; but we are ALL focused on loving and caring for each other instead of trying to cheat and beat each other!

What if this way of life spreads across the nation and around the world?

I'd sure like to find out! How about you?

I've put this out to the world, and I will continue to SUFFER and talk, write, and help whoever I can, whenever I can!

Let us let our lives, successes, and HAPPINESS be our testimony, sales pitch, and recruitment tool!

If someone asks about the changes in the way you act, or the sudden rise in your success and performance, tell them what's going on and PASS THIS BOOK ON! Yes, GIVE IT TO WHOEVER COULD USE IT!

Sure, I like money, but it's way more important to help someone learn to be happy and successful, than it is for me to have a few more dollars in my pocket.

Money won't make me happy. I'm already happy!

Please take my love and affection with you wherever you go, and come back to me whenever you want! Through this book and my website, I will always be here when you want to check in!

I send you **HUGS** and I wish you every joy and blessing this life has to offer! :)

Sincerely,

Steve

"Many of life's failures are people who did not realize how close they were to success when they gave up."

-Thomas A. Edison

Chapter 15 — Maintenance

If you're here, you're struggling and want some help getting yourself CLEAR 2 LEARN and back on track! Good! That's what this chapter is for!

Jump to whatever section applies to you! They're very similar, but they address different issues. Most of the problems we have come from unrealistic expectations!

We are too hard on ourselves and others! We try to have INTEGRITY and think we should never mess up again, but that's never going to be true! We will all make mistakes! We will all mess up from time to time!

If you're afraid you REALLY messed up, or you're ready to give up, it's okay! You're human! You're A GOOD PERSON and we all need a little help along the way! I've included some issues that I've seen my students deal with and I hope my responses will be a benefit to you! Read these if or when they apply to you!

Instead of thumbing through the pages, you can use the index here and jump to the topic you need right now. You can also go back to the Table of Contents in the front and go to the chapter you want to reread and relearn.

I'm proud of you for reading this far or coming back because you're feeling stuck!

Brutal Kindness Help Topics Index

"I HATE THAT PERSON!"

"I'm DONE with him/her!"

I'm sure you have good reasons to be angry! People who don't know what we know about DRAGGING and being MAD are usually acting the way they do because they've been CONDITIONED to expect others to argue and be upset with them and they're used to conflict!

Some of my students get in trouble again and again and don't even realize it's their own actions that are causing most of their problems. I can't do anything for them right now, so let's focus on you! Remember,

YOU'RE A GOOD PERSON! Let's go through the steps: It's time to get CLEAR2LEARN!

I HATE THAT PERSON! I'm DONE with him/her!

What happened? Explain.
Why did that get you so upset? Explain.

What/who needs to be FORGIVEN? Explain.
GREAT! You're DONE!

Now it's time to FORGIVE whatever you wrote about above: SMILE and SUFFER if you need to!

If you're REALLY not ready to do that yet, that's okay! Go back and read over the chapter on FORGIVENESS. Remember, you don't need to feel like forgiving: YOU KNOW HOW TO SUFFER! Like me, your mind has probably been conditioned to DRAG! It's time to ACT RIGHT, SUFFER, SMILE, and FORGIVE so you can think clearly!

The Practice of PURPOSEFUL FORGIVENESS

1. **SMILE (yes, SUFFER and fake it if you have to!)**

2. PUT *YOUR HAND ON YOUR HEART* and think about something this person has done, and how this person has acted.... Ready? GOOD!
3. SAY THE WORDS: "I forgive _____ for _____ and for being .... (Tell how that person was acting; it could be something like being a bully, a wimp, lazy or bossy, etc....)
4. Repeat the above FORGIVENESS statement as many times as you need to with any other issues or people you're upset about/with!
5. If you have faith in a higher power, you can also ask God to forgive that person, too!
6. SAY THE WORDS (optional)
7. "I pray and ask God to forgive me/her/him, too."
8. Take a deep breath
9. Close your hand into a fist
10. Swing your fist out in front of you
11. Say, "as I hope (and pray) to be forgiven, so will I forgive."
12. Open your hand palm up to the sky and
13. Symbolically release whatever you've been holding onto
14. Take some more deep breaths.

EXCELLENT! If you left someone off, be sure and go back and do it again! Even if you have to do it twenty or more times, keep going until you've forgiven it all!

Okay, so now that you're CLEAR 2 LEARN! It's time to think about what you can do differently. YOU'RE A GOOD PERSON, so write about it here:

What can you do to make this situation better?

What can you do different if this problem comes up again?

Done? Super COOL!

Now is a great time to do some POSITIVE AFFIRMATIONS!

Today is a GOOD DAY! Say our standard affirmations and write in your own AFFIRMATIONS and say them as often as you need to!

"I LOVE BEING SUCCESSFUL! It makes me HAPPY!"
"I LOVE BEING SMART! It makes me HAPPY!"
"I AM HEALTHY, HAPPY, AND STRONG!"
Now create POSITIVE AFFIRMATIONS that will help you! Do you feel angry? Sad? Tell about what you want as if it's what you ARE and what you LOVE! Maybe strong? Kind? Calm? In charge? Turn the page and write whatever will help YOU!

I LOVE being…
It makes me HAPPY!
I AM…

If you haven't done them yet, SUFFER, SMILE, and do the rest of your daily HABITS FOR HAPPINESS.

If you feel clear and balanced, and BACK ON TRACK, GOOD! Have a GREAT DAY! Consider sharing what you've learned with people you know who could use it! Upload a video, picture, or write about it on social media!
   #BrutalKindness

If not, go on to another help section!

-I don't think I'm doing it right!

-I don't think this is working!

-I quit!

If you're here you're probably VERY frustrated right now because things aren't going right. Whether your upset comes from yourself or someone else's mess up, you're at that point where you're ready to quit, and I'm glad you came here first instead of just throwing in the towel.

First of all, it's okay to be upset! All emotions have their place, and if we learn to channel that energy, we can turn our negative emotions into positive changes!

Secondly, be aware that when we're upset, it's easy to see all the negative and none of the positive! We focus in on the one day we failed, and ignore the many days we were happy and successful.

Thirdly, remember that because of our years of conditioning, our minds use our STRONG emotions to push us back to our old normal ways and habits. If you're feeling VERY angry, sad, etc... please put off making any BIG decisions until you're calm and CLEAR 2 LEARN.

Finally, keep in mind, ANY upset is a huge opportunity for growth and for building mental muscle! Learning to ACT RIGHT and work through problems, instead of just getting mad and reacting, can be the stepping stone to a whole new level of happiness and success!

Alrighty, are you ready to get CLEAR 2 LEARN, regain your balance, and come up with solutions to any problems you're facing? Great, me too! If not, put this away for a while and RELAX! Get some exercise, go for a walk, call a friend. Come back whenever you're ready. This book will still be here!

Okay, ready? Good!

Think about why you're so upset. Maybe...

- Somebody did something that reminds of a situation you were in before and you're mad as if this was a continuation of that past event.
- You're mad at the same person AGAIN because he or she messed up AGAIN, and you're fed up!
- Everything seems to be going wrong and nothing you do is right.
- People seem to be going out of their way to annoy you.

Regardless of what you're upset about, the best thing you can do is get those thoughts out of your head and onto paper!

Write about what you're upset about and go through the steps below. **If what you're upset about involves abuse or illegal activity, please seek help immediately!**

Turn the page to Write and Reflect: I don't think I'm doing it right! I don't think this is working! I quit!

What are you upset about? Explain.

How does it make you feel? Explain.

How old do you feel and what does this particular upset remind you of? Explain.

Who and/or what needs to be FORGIVEN? (from the past and today!) Explain.

What else needs to be said and/or FORGIVEN? Explain

EXCELLENT! I hope this helped! Remember, YOU'RE A GOOD PERSON!

It's okay to feel bad and still ACT RIGHT!

Now it's time to FORGIVE whatever you wrote about.

The Practice of PURPOSEFUL FORGIVENESS

1. **SMILE (yes, SUFFER and fake it if you have to!)**
2. **PUT *YOUR HAND ON YOUR HEART* and think about something this person has done, and how this person has acted.... Ready? GOOD!**
3. **SAY THE WORDS: "I forgive _____ for _____ and for being .... (Tell how that person was acting; it could be something like being a bully, a wimp, lazy or bossy, etc....)**
4. **Repeat the Above FORGIVENESS statement as many times as you need to with any other issues or people you're upset about/with!**
5. **If you have faith in a higher power, you can also ask God to forgive that person, too!**
6. **SAY THE WORDS (optional)**
7. **"I pray and ask God to forgive me/her/him, too."**

8. Take a deep breath
9. Close your hand into a fist
10. Swing your fist out in front of you
11. Say, "as I hope (and pray) to be forgiven, so will I forgive."
12. Open your hand palm up to the sky and
13. Symbolically release whatever you've been holding onto
14. Take some more deep breaths.

EXCELLENT! If you left someone off, be sure and go back and do it again! Even if you have to do it twenty or more times, keep going until you've FORGIVEN it all!

If you feel like someone has repeatedly wronged you, be sure and FORGIVE YOURSELF for letting this continue! No, I'm not saying it's your fault, but getting hurt and getting upset can become automatic! Forgiving yourself can help you bring that pattern to an end!

Okay, so now that you're CLEAR 2 LEARN! It's time to think about what you can do differently. YOU'RE A GOOD PERSON, so write about it here:

What can I do to make this situation better? Explain.

What can I do differently if this same problem comes up again? Explain.

| |
| |
| |
| |

Super COOL!

Now is a great time to do some POSITIVE AFFIRMATIONS!

Today is a GOOD DAY! Read mine and/or write in your AFFIRMATIONS and say them as often as you need to!

| "I LOVE BEING SMART! It makes me HAPPY!" |
| "I LOVE BEING SUCCESSFUL! It makes me HAPPY!" |
| Now create your own POSITIVE AFFIRMATIONS: Tell what you ARE and what you LOVE! Maybe patient? Kind? Calm? In charge? Write whatever will help YOU! |
| I AM... |
| |
| I AM... |
| |
| I LOVE... |
| It makes me HAPPY! |
| I LOVE... |
| It makes me HAPPY! |

I hope you feel better and if not, that's okay, too! At least now you have a game plan you can follow if you're in a similar situation and feel like this again! Do your other daily HABITS FOR HAPPINESS if you haven't done them today.

Q-What if I keep having the same problem, or a bad memory keeps coming up again and again?

A-Then you FORGIVE it over and over again! I have to FORGIVE the same upsets from the past over and over again, too! Also, without ever meaning to, I put myself in situations that make me feel the way I remember from my old normal way of life. That's right, I'm talking about conditioning!

When I was young, I saw myself as a weak failure; and from time to time I still have to FORGIVE myself for that, too, and my father for being a mean jerk. I FORGIVE so I can let it go and get back to my NEW NORMAL way of life!

When I tell people that my past still haunts me, they're usually shocked! They say, "oh no! You shouldn't feel that way!" I just smile and shrug and keep doing what I know is right. Trying not to think or not feel something is a hopeless task! I'm much better off feeling what I feel and FORGIVING whatever I remember than trying not to feel or not think about it! The same is probably true for you, too!

If you feel clear and ready to get back to your NEW NORMAL, great! You can upload a picture or video, or write about it on social media!   #BrutalKindness

If you feel you would benefit from more coaching or thought on the matter, please continue on to the next help topic!

Either way, I'm sending you a **HUG** through this book! :)

-Something REALLY BAD happened!

-People ALWAYS treat me BAD!

-Why do BAD things ALWAYS happen to me!

If you are concerned for your health or well-being, or fear you may harm yourself or others, please see a mental health professional immediately! If you are under the care of a mental health professional, follow his or her advice, NOT mine! I am neither a mental health professional nor a doctor!

Okay. If you're here, then you must be having a really hard time. I'm sorry you're having to deal with this. Right now, you may not be in the mood to do your affirmations or be positive on purpose.

That's okay! You don't have to!

Life can be VERY HARD. People die, disappoint us, mistreat us, leave us; and sometimes BAD things just happen! It's all over the news and, if you watch too much, you could easily feel like the world is a VERY BAD place.

But **it doesn't have to be unless you decide it is!** The world is what you make of it. When really bad things happen to us, we feel so overwhelmed that we can become emotionally crippled. We're too sad, too mad, too hurt, too upset, and then things start to fall apart because we can't deal with the everyday stresses and problems of life. We fall behind in work or school, we isolate ourselves from friends and family, and maybe we even start to think that this life isn't worth living.

BAD things happen to ALL OF US sooner or later! I've had my share, too!

My father's death, the end of my first marriage and my divorce, and my son's health problems, and my mother's slow decline and death all left me feeling broken and hopeless.

We feel like we can't move forward and nothing will ever make us feel better, but remember that our FEELINGS ARE NOT THE TRUTH and they won't stay the same for very long!

Here's the important thing to remember about HARD TIMES! We get to decide what they mean! Strong emotions will eventually fade and how you ACT during and after a difficult time or shake up can have a huge effect on your future!

Yes, HARD TIMES can destroy you! You can decide that this is too much and hold onto your memories like gashes in your emotional and mental skin that never heal. You can feel wounded, stay wounded, and never recover!

But, you can also decide that HARD TIMES MAKE YOU STRONG! You can FORGIVE, LEARN, and GET BACK ON TRACK! You can become wiser, kinder, more understanding. You can use that wisdom to be a blessing to those around you! Because you've learned how to work through those hard times, you can teach others how to do the same! **That's the main reason why this book got written and is in your hands!**

The question is are you going to live happy and well because you're going to make the best of what you have, or are you going to live sad and small because you've been hurt before and won't risk being hurt again?

If right now, you just CAN'T see the positive and can't deal with it. It's okay! I would suggest just doing ONE THING!

SUFFER, ACT RIGHT, and thank or compliment someone who's been good to you no matter how you feel!

SERIOUSLY, DO IT! NOW!

Doing just that one POSITIVE thing can create an opening that will help you see that your emotions are NOT the truth. Then, if you want to, continue and do your next daily HABIT FOR HAPPINESS. SUFFER if you have to! You're worth it!

Ready to work through your upset? GOOD! Let's move on!

It's time to Reflect: -Something REALLY BAD happened and I don't know what to do! -People ALWAYS treat me BAD! -Why do BAD things ALWAYS happen to me?

So, tell what happened. Write what you remember, what you feel, what you think!

What happened? Explain.

Why are you so upset? Explain.

Why do you think this happened? Explain.

What did you learn about yourself and others? Explain.

EXCELLENT! You got it done on paper, in your head, or you skipped it! The choice is ALWAYS yours!

Okay, so now it's time to FORGIVE! Remember, you're FORGIVING FOR YOU! You're FORGIVING so you can move forward in your life!

If you're upset about something that happens again and again, or someone keeps hurting you over and over, be sure and forgive **YOURSELF** for letting them! Yes, it's someone else's fault for taking advantage of you, but if you've been conditioned to see yourself as a victim, it could become a pattern for you that you repeat without even knowing it. It definitely is a pattern for me, and until I forgave myself, I kept finding myself in those same negative situations!

By forgiving yourself, you're letting go of whatever made you see yourself as something other than strong, so then you can get back to your NEW NORMAL!

If you're still not ready to FORGIVE, that's okay! Put this aside and come back when you've had time to cool off! Or do your daily HABITS FOR HAPPINESS! SUFFERING and ACTING RIGHT and going through your NEW NORMAL routine can help you start to think though and work through your emotions!

Now it's time to FORGIVE whatever you wrote on the previous page: (Add in or leave off God as you feel is appropriate!)

The Practice of PURPOSEFUL FORGIVENESS

1. **SMILE (yes, SUFFER and fake it if you have to!)**

2. PUT *YOUR HAND ON YOUR HEART* and think about something this person has done, and how this person has acted…. Ready? GOOD!
3. SAY THE WORDS: "I forgive _____ for _____ and for being …. (Tell how that person was acting; it could be something like being a bully, a wimp, lazy or bossy, etc.…)
4. Repeat the Above FORGIVENESS statement as many times as you need to with any other issues or people you're upset about/with!
5. If you have faith in a higher power, you can also ask God to forgive that person, too!
6. SAY THE WORDS (optional)
7. "I pray and ask God to forgive me/her/him, too."
8. Take a deep breath
9. Close your hand into a fist
10. Swing your fist out in front of you
11. Say, "as I hope (and pray) to be forgiven, so will I forgive."
12. Open your hand palm up to the sky and
13. Symbolically release whatever you've been holding onto
14. Take some more deep breaths.

EXCELLENT! Do it again as many times as you need to until you've FORGIVEN everything you're upset about, and you feel CLEAR 2 LEARN!

Now, it's time to problem solve! Be **BRUTALLY KIND** and SUFFER if you have to! Care enough to ACT RIGHT and do the work necessary to help yourself regain your balance!

Okay, so now that you're not so upset anymore, it's time to write about what you can do differently. YOU'RE A GOOD PERSON, so write about it here:

What can you do NOW to make this situation better? Explain.
What can you do differently if this problem, situation, or kind of person comes up in your life again? Explain.

Are you still struggling or skipping steps? Read the Q&A on the next page as needed!

BRUTAL KINDNESS Q&A:

Q-"Why should I forgive myself because someone else was a jerk? Forgive myself because someone took advantage of me? That's WRONG! I didn't do anything!"

A-If you feel strongly about it, then do what's best for you!

If you're currently in an abusive situation, get help! Call the National Domestic Abuse Hotline at 1-800-799-7233!

But here's why I think it's important to FORGIVE yourself when others mistreat you: we can become conditioned to being treated bad! If you have a history of being treated bad, especially if there was abuse or neglect in your childhood, it may now be part of your old normal conditioning and you may come to expect it, be drawn to it, and even do things to make it happen. **NO, NOT ON PURPOSE, and NO, I DIDN'T SAY YOU LIKED IT!** But if you're conditioned to be a victim, you may find yourself drawn towards people who are conditioned to act like bullies or predators!

Forgiving yourself for being a victim means it's easier to recognize what you're doing and stand up for yourself sooner! It means you'll have a much greater chance of noticing when you're about to put yourself in an unhealthy situation and do something different **BECAUSE YOU CARE!**

If the abuse from the past is still haunting you, then forgive that abuser as well as yourself! I have to FORGIVE my father again and again! You may have to do the same thing!

Remember, people who FORGIVE are STRONG! Your ACTIONS prove to you who you really are, so if or when you're faced with a similar situation, the strength you're building now will allow you to see things differently and ACT differently!

That's what helps me when I meet people or have students who are extremely rude or mean! I used to see myself as weak, so in a confrontation I'd usually back down. Even now, if I find myself dealing with someone like Dad, I automatically think, "it's okay, no big deal. I shouldn't say anything."

Instead of just backing down, I address the problem! Now, because I've FORGIVEN myself for feeling like a weak victim and Dad for being a mean jerk, I'll stop and think again! I'll stand up for myself and speak up for myself. I'll talk to that person calmly, instead of getting into an argument like I used to with Dad, and help that person figure out why they're acting that way and help them learn to ACT differently, too!

And yes, if they really are bent on acting like a jerk, I WILL NOT PUT UP WITH IT! Many people will not respect you until you prove that you respect yourself enough to stand up for yourself. Usually, I have to only write a student up once, and then he or she will realize that I will not be taken advantage of or disrespected! I often have to SUFFER to do it, but I don't let people walk all over me very often anymore!

If I do mess up, I FORGIVE, LEARN, AND GET BACK ON TRACK right away instead of letting things continue to get worse!

Changing how you ACT and respond to people might also mean that because you speak up sooner and demand better treatment, the same person who would normally act like a bully around you will act differently, too! Your strength and self-respect makes others respect you, as well!

In most cases, the key to stopping bullying isn't just to punish the bullies, but for ALL OF US to learn how to have INTEGRITY and DO WHAT'S RIGHT NO MATTER HOW WE FEEL!

Q-"What if there's nobody to forgive? What if something bad just happened?"

A-If something tragic happened like a fire, death, bad accident, an earthquake, cancer or other serious illness, you may have to forgive GOD, too!

Yes, I know, **GOD DOESN'T NEED OUR FORGIVENESS**, but sometimes we NEED to FORGIVE bad luck, fate, or even God so we can get ourselves back in balance.

Think about it for a moment and forgive God if you're holding onto feelings like, "how can God let something like this happen?" or "if there is a God, he sure doesn't give a damn about us!"

I've felt both those ways before, and forgiving God was like dropping a hundred-pound weight off my shoulders. Do what's best for you!

You can also create a NEW NORMAL AFFIRMATION like "I love being strong and independent! It makes me HAPPY!"

"I am strong, smart, and good."

"People love and respect me and I respect myself."

If your mind cringes away from even reading those words, then your emotions are still very charged! You can do it anyway! FORGIVE YOURSELF for feeling stuck and do it anyway! The only you'll start to become comfortable acting strong is to start changing the soundtrack in your head! I've had to do just that many times!

DON'T WAIT TO FEEL LIKE IT! SUFFER, HAVE INTEGRITY AND ACT RIGHT! Say the AFFIRMATIONS below!

"I love being strong and independent! It makes me HAPPY!"
"I am strong, smart, and good."
"People love and respect me, and I respect myself."
EXCELLENT! I'm proud of you for ACTING RIGHT no matter how you feel!
Now create POSITIVE AFFIRMATIONS that will you help you: Tell what you ARE and what you LOVE! Maybe healthy? Strong? Calm? In charge? Write whatever will help YOU!
I AM...

I AM...
I LOVE...
It makes me HAPPY!
I LOVE...
It makes me HAPPY!

If you were too emotional, MAD, or DRAGGING to do the writing before, go back and fill them in now! FORGIVE each person or situation on the list. You may have to say the words again and again before you actually feel your emotions letting go and your heart and mind feel FORGIVENESS!

I'm so proud of you! You're on your way to becoming a STRONG, HEALTHY, HAPPY, SUCCESSFUL, GOOD PERSON!

Remember, you can always revisit a chapter, these help topics, or find more info and helpful videos on my website: clear2learn.net

Remember, YOU'RE A GOOD PERSON!

Bye for now!

:)

Steve

About the Author:

Steven Carvajal is happily married with five grown children, most of whom still live with us....I mean him. After spending four years working for a credit card company and, twenty years working in the grocery business, he had a conversation with his boss.

She asked, "Are you closing manager tonight?"

He replied, "Yes, I am." He smiled and continued, "Why? Is it because I do such a good job?"

She shook her head, "No... I mean, yes, you do a good job; but honestly I love reading your emails. YOU'RE SO FUNNY! You're telling me about everything that happened that night and I'm just sitting there cracking up the whole time!"

He smiled, shrugged, and said, "Thanks! I do have a degree in English."

She did a double-take. "Really?"

"Yes."

Then she looked at him, really looked at him and said, "What are you doing here? You should be a teacher! Look how these kids all listen to you and jump to do what you ask them to do."

He looked down, turning red, but she continued anyway.

"Seriously! Your talent is being wasted here."

He'd thought about it before, but that AFFIRMATION of his talent and ability was what he needed to make that change!

It was the best thing he ever did!

Thank you, Susan Warthen, for giving me the push I needed!

:)

-Steve

148

Made in the USA
Lexington, KY
30 October 2019